P9-AQV-504

PALATINE CHURCH VISITATIONS, 1609

Deanery of Kusel

PALATINE CHURCH VISITATIONS, 1609

Deanery of Kusel

Translated by Ricardo W. Staudt

With a Note by Hermann Friedrich Macco

&

NEW INTRODUCTION

By Don Yoder

CLEARFIELD COMPANY
REPRINTS & REMAINDERS

Reprinted for Clearfield Company Inc. by
Genealogical Publishing Co. Inc.
Baltimore, MD 1990

Originally published as a Special Number of the
*Publications of the Genealogical Society of
Pennsylvania*, August, 1930.
Reprinted, with a New Introduction, by
Genealogical Publishing Co., Inc.
Baltimore, 1980
Copyright © 1980
Genealogical Publishing Co., Inc.
Baltimore, Maryland
All Rights Reserved
Library of Congress Catalogue Card Number 80-68128
International Standard Book Number 0-8063-0908-3
Made in the United States of America

INTRODUCTION

H ERBERT HOOVER was President of the United States in
1930 when a curious and intricate international genealogical project linking the Palatinate and Pennsylvania led to the publication by the Genealogical Society of
Pennsylvania of the work which is here being reissued—
Palatine Church Visitations, 1609.

The connection between President Hoover and the present
work lies in the fact that a wealthy Argentine-German
exporter named Ricardo W. Staudt, of Buenos Aires, in the
1920's had hired the German genealogist, Dr. Hermann
Friedrich Macco, to find, among other lineages, the Palatine
ancestry of Herbert Hoover. Hoover was the first President
of the United States to bear a non-British Isles name and to
represent, at least in part of his ancestry, the great wave of
German immigration to the United States. In the course of
this research, which covered large areas of the Palatinate, a
document was discovered in the Archive of the Protestant
Church in the town of Konken, near Kusel, in the western
part of the Palatinate, dating from the beginning of the
seventeenth century. This was the Church Visitation Book
for the Deanery of Kusel for the year 1609. It listed the total
population of the area in that year, by families, with names,
occupations, and relationships. Included were a great many
villages in the Kusel area. Each of the major centers, parishes in the state church system, contained smaller villages,
to a total of 113 separate localities. Certain missing portions
of the book, dealing with the parish of Niederkirchen and its
dependencies, were discovered in the Church Archive at
Niederkirchen, rounding out the documentation.

Church Visitations were practiced in both the Catholic
and Protestant worlds. They were official ecclesiastical inves-
tigations into the status of the local churches, the local minis-
try, the church buildings, and the people and their morality.
They contain complaints by the clergy and in some cases
complaints about the clergy. As such they provide dated
materials on the local scene, with pointed references to what
was wrong in the parish at a certain time in history. Since
the information was collected for the most part on the basis
of interviews, visitation reports can be considered an early
example of what we now call oral history. What makes
this particular visitation record distinctive is its inclu-
sion of family registers for each parish and each village
investigated.

For Americans researching the backgrounds of their emigrant Palatine ancestry, these family registers—from 1609, a full century before the mass migration to the New World—are a primary and useful aid. As Dr. Macco suggests in his brief preface, "considering the permanent residency of the Palatine peasants, the proof that the name occurs in a certain parish will be sufficient to trace the emigrated man and his descent." This is certainly true of the more unusual surnames represented in this list which turn up as well among the colonial German population of the United States. For an example, the Staudt families of Eastern Pennsylvania trace their lineage to emigrants from Wolfersweiler and adjoining villages in the Kusel area. Other such families, represented both in this list and in the Strassburger-Hinke *Pennsylvania German Pioneers,* include: Bollenbacher, Hobacker, Hutmacher, Laufferweiler, Ladenberg, Lawer, Matzenbacher, Morgenstern, Schmeyer, Selbacher, Steinhausen, Strohschneider, Theisinger, Wollenweber, Wernig, Winkenbacher, and Windringer. There are of course many others.

A factor heightening the value of this work for emigration genealogy is the existence of two published lists which contain the names of eighteenth-century emigrants from the same area. These are (1) William John Hinke and John Baer Stoudt, "A List of German Immigrants to the American Colonies from Zweibruecken in the Palatinate, 1728-1749," in *The Pennsylvania German Folklore Society,* I (1936), 101-124, reprinted in *Pennsylvania German Immigrants, 1709-1786,* ed. Don Yoder (Baltimore, 1980), pp. 289-312; and (2) "A List of German Immigrants to the American Colonies from Zweibruecken in the Palatinate, 1750-1771," edited by Friedrich Krebs, with introduction by Don Yoder, in *The Pennsylvania German Folklore Society,* XVI (1951), 171-183, reprinted in *Pennsylvania German Immigrants, 1709-1786,* pp. 313-325.

To illustrate the value of the Palatine Church Visitation List of 1609 for emigration research, take the single example of the Diehl family of Southeastern Pennsylvania. According to the Hinke-Stoudt Zweibruecken emigration list, cited above, at least seven emigrants by this name came to America in the eighteenth century, some with their families, from the three adjacent villages of Hinzweiler, Oberweiler, and Horschbach, all in the St. Julian area of the Glan Valley in the West Central Palatinate. For example, the records left by the Zweibruecken officialdom tell us that *Michel Diehl* of Hinzweiler "leaves for America" (1741); *Simon Peter Dhiel* of Hinzweiler "leaves for America" (1742); *Simon Jakob Diel* of Oberweiler, *Jakob Dhiel* and his brother *Wilhelm*

Dhiel of Horspach, all "leave for America" (1742) ; and *Daniel Dhiel* of Oberweiler, with wife and six children, along with *Philip Dhiel* of Horspach, single, leave for the same destination (1744).

Checking these towns in the Visitation List we come up with the following connection. Hinzweiler in 1609 had twenty "hearths" (i.e. households), Oberweiler thirty-four hearths, and Horspach (now Horschbach) thirteen hearths. While no Diehls were listed as resident in Hinzweiler in 1609, the other two villages contained several. There were, for example, two families of Diehls in Oberweiler. *Johannes Diel* was obviously the chief inhabitant since he was listed first and his titles are given in Latin as "Scabinus Censor et juratus." With him were his wife *Verina, Carolus* his servant, and *Elisabeth* his maid. His occupation was farmer, as was No. 14, *Abraham Diel,* with *Elisabeth* his wife, sons *Jacob, Elias,* and *Sebastian,* and daughters *Margreta, Anna, Elisabeth,* and *Martha.* At nearby Horschbach in 1609 lived (No. 8) *Daniel Diel,* with *Anna* his wife, sons *Johan, Jacob,* and *Hans,* and daughters *Margreta* and *Elisabeth;* (No. 12) *Jacob Diel,* with his wife *Engel* and *Margretha* a servant; also (No. 13) *Johannes Diel,* with *Barbara* his wife, sons *Noha* and *Tobias,* and daughters *Anna Maria* and *Elisabeth.* Finally, there was the widower *Peter Diel,* member of the village council, living in the household of (No. 1) *Johan Moor,* village magistrate, and his family.

Obviously this nest of Diehls in the Western Palatinate produced the emigrants who carried the family name to the New World over a century and a quarter later. American genealogists can undoubtedly connect the emigrant generations with the families of 1609 by means of the church registers for Hinzweiler, which begin in 1637, and those for Oberweiler, which begin in 1640. An exciting prospect indeed for those tracing their Palatine roots!

2

The two persons responsible for making the *Palatine Church Visitations* of 1609 available to the genealogical world deserve biographical notice here. Dr. Hermann Friedrich Macco (1864-1945) of Berlin, was the son of Dr. Heinrich Macco (1843-1920) of Siegen in Westphalia, civil engineer and European authority on mining economics, the iron industry, and railroad systems. From 1876 to 1903 he made several research trips to the United States, during which he investigated American iron production and railroad networks, and wrote and lectured widely about them. The son was a historian who wrote several basic books on the history of the Imperial City of Aachen. But his major interest was genealogy. His most celebrated work in Germany, apart from individual family histories (Peltze, Pastor, and others), was the two-volume treatise *Aachener Wappen und Genealogien: Ein Beitrag zur Wappenkunde und Genealogie Aachener, Limburgischer und Jülicher Familien* (Aachen, 1907-1908). Among his last labors was the multi-volume typescript, *Swiss Emigrants to the Palatinate in Germany and to America 1650-1800 and Huguenots in the Palatinate and Germany*, arranged and indexed by the Genealogical Society of the Church of Jesus Christ of Latter-day Saints, Salt Lake City, Utah, 1954.

Ricardo W. Staudt (1888-1955) was a native of Berlin, but from an Argentine-German merchant family, his father, Guillermo Jacobo Staudt having been born in the Argentine in 1852. After university studies in Germany and France, Ricardo Staudt headed the firm of Staudt and Company, founded by his father, shipping wool, hides, leather, beef, and other agricultural products of Argentina all over the world. In addition, he was director of various industries, banks, and cultural institutions in Argentina. His scholarly interests included the genealogical sciences, and he wrote several works in Spanish on European genealogy. But since his own Staudt ancestry involved the Palatinate, he became interested in the fact that Staudts had emigrated to America in the 1730's from Wolfersweiler and other villages in the Kusel area in the Western Palatinate. He became acquainted with the Reverend Dr. John Baer Stoudt, Reformed minister in Eastern Pennsylvania, and joined forces with him to search European archives for Staudt family data.

The product of this collaboration was *The Staudt-Stoudt-Stout-Family of Pennsylvania and Their Ancestors in the Palatinate: A Preliminary Study* (n.p., 1925). The section on "The Staudt Ancestors in the Palatinate" was "presented to his American kinsfolk at their thirteenth family reunion," by Ricardo W. Staudt, with a preface addressed "Dear Kinfolks." The preface acknowledged the help of Dr. Macco, then of Berlin-Stieglitz, "who has been at work for many years for that part of the Staudt Family still in Germany."

Because of his interest in Pennsylvania German genealogy, Ricardo Staudt was elected a life member of the Genealogical Society of Pennsylvania in 1928. In November of that year he sent an article to the Society which turns out to be the present work. The Report of the Executive Committee on 15 October 1929 gives details. "At an expenditure of considerable time, money and knowledge, Mr. Staudt has collected the Palatinate Church Visitation Records of the Deanery of Kusel for 1609 . . . . These he has arranged and translated so that his manuscript is in complete shape for printing. This he gives to the Society for publication." The Wickersham Printing Company of Lancaster estimated the cost of printing an edition of 650 copies at about $500.00, of which half was generously donated by the editor.

At the same time the Visitation List was being processed, the team of Staudt-Macco collaborated also in researching the ancestry of President Hoover. Staudt's preliminary article, "The Story of a Research upon the Origin of the Huber-Hoover Families in the Palatinate," *National Genealogical Society Quarterly*, XVII:1 (March 1929), apparently went off on the wrong track, focusing on the wrong emigrant Andreas Huber. On the American side of the Atlantic, Colonel Calvin I. Kephart had begun an independent search, but both Staudt and Kephart eventually fastened upon the correct Andreas Huber, of Ellerstadt, who emigrated to Philadelphia in 1738 and went on to North Carolina. Staudt went on, with Macco's help, to elaborate on his own Huber ancestry in the thorough article, "The Huber-Hoover Family of Aesch, Switzerland and Trippstadt, Palatinate, with some Accent on Migrations to Pennsylvania," in *Publications of the Genealogical Society of Pennsylvania*, XII:3 (March 1935), 223-243. This international controversy over the President's ancestry, a tempest in the genealogical teapot of the 1920's and 1930's, is summarized in Hulda Hoover McLean, *Genealogy of the Herbert Hoover Family* (Stanford, California, 1967).

3

The Palatine Visitation List was translated by Ricardo Staudt, whose English was almost impeccable. Only occasionally did he fail to translate something, as for example (p. 5) *reysiger im ausschuss* (cavalryman) ; (p. 34) *weilerischer meier* (tenant on the village farm) ; (p. 36) *keller* (not "cellarman" but rather a local official of the Palatinate government, short for *Amtskeller*) ; (p. 42) *Göltzer* (castrator) ; (p. 43) *Bruchschneider* (hernia doctor) ; and (p. 44) *der alt Bott* (the old courier). The frequent term *Schöffe* (*Schöpfen, Scheffen*) refers to a kind of under-magistrate or juryman who assists a local judge; for example, the *Schöffengericht* is the local village court, with a petty judge and two jurymen or lay assessors. In addition, the translator leaves to our imagination several intriguing phrases. The first of these is (p. 38) "Maria, the 'schwerer' widow"—was she pregnant or just clumsy or difficult? Or, using Palatine dialect, was she simply the mother-in-law of Velten Bauch,

ix

in whose household she resided in Deckenhart? Another woman (p. 40) "serves on the Gauw"—was she a member of the county tribunal, the petty sessions? This would have been highly unlikely in the seventeenth century when village women had to keep their place in a man's world. More likely she was a servant of one of the district officials. At any rate these are a few places where for exact translation one needs a knowledge of both local Palatine German and of historical Palatine governmental terminology.

But there is another problem avoided in many but not all cases by the translator. After page 8 he occasionally leaves the occupational designations in the original Latin. For readers whose knowledge of archival Latin is minimal or non-existent, it is perhaps well to present here a glossary of the occupational terms and other terms in Latin left untranslated.

agricola	= farmer
bubulcus	= ploughman, or herdsman
caupo	= small shopkeeper, innkeeper
censor	= magistrate
coriarius	= tanner
chirurgus	= surgeon
faber	= blacksmith
faber ferrarius	= blacksmith
faber armamentarius	= armorer
figulus	= potter
juror	= juryman, assistant judge in village court
lanificus	= woolweaver or wool processor
lanius	= butcher
lapicida	= stonecutter
lignarius	= carpenter
mechanicus	= mechanic
mendicus	= beggar
miles	= soldier
molitor	= builder
negociator	= wholesaler, trader
operarius	= day laborer
ovium pastor	= shepherd
pistor	= miller
propola	= huckster
praetor	= magistrate
praetor nobilis	= magistrate belonging to a magistrate family, i.e. not a newcomer to office or of ignoble family
sartor	= tailor

scabinus	= magistrate, bailiff
	(German *Schöffen*)
scrivarius	= clerk
senator	= member of the village council
sutor	= shoemaker, cobbler
textor	= weaver
vietor	= cooper

In addition, there are certain Latin phrases left untranslated in the text. For example, *ecclesiastes Conckanus* (p. 46) means "clergyman of Konken;" *homo senex annorum 105* (p. 53) = "old man aged 105;" *conjux ob delicta in exilio* (p. 17) = "husband in exile on account of crimes;" *ex papatu* (p. 34) = "of the papacy," i.e. Roman Catholic; *in the week post cantate* (p. 5) = "in the week after Cantate Sunday," i.e. the fourth Sunday after Easter in the church year; *stude[n]t Hornba[ch]ei* = "student at Hornbach;" and *filius mente captus* (p. 19) = "feebleminded son." And, finally, some common terms for family and household relationships were left untranslated: *uxor* = "wife;" *filius* = "son;" *filia* = "daughter;" *filius coelebs* = "unmarried son;" *adoptivus* = "adopted son;" *famulus* = "manservant;" *famula* = "maidservant;" *ancilla* = "maidservant;" *conjux* = "spouse;" *nepos* = "nephew;" *viduus* = "widower;" and *vidua* = "widow." And there is also *vulgo* = "commonly known as, or nicknamed, as follows."

If the European editor set his sights too high in regard to American fluency in reading Latin, at least he provided his readers with three indispensable indexes in the book. These include: (1) Index of Parishes and Subsidiary Towns Listed in the Visitation, pp. 79-80; (2) List of Personal Names, with Derivations, as, for example, Enders (Andreas), p. 81; and (3) List of all Family Names, each with individual personal names, pp. 82-136.

In addition to its genealogical focus, the book gives us valuable insight into the village structure out of which most of our eighteenth-century emigrant ancestors came, shedding light on the family structure; the care of widows, widowers, and orphans by the family network; the governmental apparatus of the village; and the economic life with its various occupations.

In conclusion, we wish to express our thanks to the Genealogical Society of Pennsylvania for permission to reissue this special number of its publications, fifty years after its initial appearance.

University of Pennsylvania　　　　　　　　DON YODER
8 June 1980

PALATINE CHURCH—VISITATIONS
1609

THE PROTESTANT PAROCHIAL VISITATIONS.

Examinations of the internal and external conditions of the parishes by the upper church authorities are understood by the name of "parochial visitations". They already occurred in the sixth and seventh centuries and belonged to the chief functions of the bishops, who later on left this work to the archdeacons. After the Reformation, Luther laid great stress on the control of the clergymen by these visitations, and therefore recommended them to the Elector Johann of Saxonia in order to have the church affairs of his country examined. For this purpose, Philipp Melanchthon wrote the so-called "visitation-booklet".

The first Protestant parochial visitation began in 1527 and was finished two years later. Luther himself and some worldly [lay] deputies, also several theologians such as Justus Jonas, Johann Buggenhagen and Spalatin have been active in connection with this visitation. Such visitations have also been arranged by the Catholic Church authorities. Thus, for instance, in 1533 a very exact examination had been arranged in the duchy of Jülich, giving a very unfavorable picture of the morality of the clergy, as everywhere the clergymen lived together with their maid-servants from whom they often had many children. Such parochial visitations soon followed in the other parts of Germany, and official minutes were taken down about their results. Unfortunately, only very few of them are still available.

The chief purpose of these parochial visitations was to state the number of inhabitants in the various deaneries, parishes and districts. The church alterations required some evidence about the increase or decrease of the church visitors, so that the reasons could be traced if necessary, the negligent clergymen could be warned and urged to do their duty, and on the other hand an assistant could be engaged to avoid an overburdening of the clergyman in consequence of a great increase of people. Furthermore, the parochial visitations punish any breach of church discipline, observe the church customs, prevent failures of clergymen and examine their knowledge. For the latter reason, we still find in some minutes as proofs the description of the lives of the clergymen attached that fully inform us as to their origin and the course of their studies. Some historical remarks, statements about the condition of the church, the rectory and school are also of value. The visitation minutes of Zweibrücken, dated 1580, even contains exact lists of pupils, stating age and place of birth, copies of the christening registers of the whole deanery of 1579/80, birth certificates of the clergymen, documents concerning their former appointments etc.

The Palatine visitation minutes of the deanery of Kusel of the year 1609 complete the entries of the church registers by exact lists of inhabitants, arranged in families and stating the age. They are of still greater importance for those parishes that do not possess any christening, wedding or death registers of that time. The entries relating to the history of the families are often completed by adding the profession. They further offer first-class evidence for the genealogy of the emigrated families, especially of those who migrated to North America and Pennsylvania. Considering the permanent residency of the Palatine peasants, the proof that the name occurs in a certain parish will be sufficient to trace the emigrated man and his descent. Then the church registers form a safe connection to the passengers' lists of 1725-1775, issued by the Pennsylvania Archives in 1890.

The church archives of the parish Konken have among the older books a folio volume containing 202 sheets, of which the sheets 144-151 (Ohmbach), 170-171 and 178-179 (Niederkirchen) are missing. Sheet 1 begins with a "catalogue of the books in the church of Alten Glan, anno 1609" containing "an old torn bible which was formerly found in the church and was printed at Worms by Peter Schöfern in 1529". There are also some church rules by Duke Wolfgang mentioned. Then follow eight books by Luther, Melanchthon, Erasmus von Rotterdam, Johannes Brentius (Brenz) and Buggenhagen. Sheet 2 contains a " list of the annual competence and parish properties of the parish Altten Glan" out of the old competence register which the clergyman Johann Foenilius received from his predecessor in 1594. Rents of money, grains, oats [1] and wine are stated separately, and at

---

[1] Sheet 3 v. "The young noblemen who were formerly called 'street-robbers' and are now called 'Rehenherrn' give annually 5 'malter' of oats on the rent-day at Welchwiller the first Sunday after Martinmas and at Bettesbach on the next Wednesday."

last landed property, fields, "Ausfelder and Wilderung", shrubs and hedges and stock of cattle.

According to a list of the inhabitants of Altenglan and the appertaining villages, etc., there is on sheet 10 a second supplementary list of the books with theological contents, many of which are polemical pamphlets arranged in quarto and octavo size, about 80 in all, from various parts of Germany and Switzerland. Seven volumes "libri historici", fifteen "libri medici" and two "scholastici" complete this parochial library.

The list of the books and rents—the latter mostly according to older precedents — repeats itself, sheet 18-20 for Flürseappel, sheet 33-34 for Hinzweiler, sheet 53-61 for Baumholder, sheet 67-72 for Achtelsbach, sheet 84-96 for Wolfersweiler, sheet 114-116 and 172-176 for Kusel, sheet 134-139 for Konken and sheet 154-155 for Pfeffelbach.

Many complaints of the clergymen are of ethical importance for the civilization. The clergyman Johannes Sibelius of Flürseappel complains of the poor attendance at church, that people are always going to the inns and have great "family feasts or dinners".[1] Sibelius further rails at the young people for roaming from village to village during Lent with violins and whistles, not only "to beg for roast meat and eggs" but "to attract maids and women and spend the whole night with eating, drinking and dancing which engendered other vices such as fornication and wantonness as examples have shown." He continues: "I have rebuked from the pulpit with great severity and christian zeal, but they did not obey." Also in the parish Hinzweiler the clergyman Jeremias Lintz blames the expensive "family dinners" which only rich people can now afford. The clergyman Martin Hoffiûs, Cuselanus, of Wolfersweiler, has written a most remarkable "List of the competence of the parochial service of Wolffersweiler, anno 1609" which refers to a precedent of 1586 by the Kirchenschaffner and Keller" Johann Wernichius and Michel Richter of Nohfelden. This contains the following remark: "When the banns of marriage are declared in church, 6 albus are due to the clergyman pro proclamatione. When there is a marriage and the couple is wedded, they owe the clergyman a meal, mèat and roast meat, 6 albus' worth, also one quart of

[1] Fol. 97 contains the remark "that often 100 persons were asked for such a dinner."

wine and 4 loaves such as are baked for the wedding break-
fast. These should be applied for and fetched for the clergyman by the bell-ringer. The former shall then give him in
return one of the four loaves. When a child is christened, the
family used to invite the clergyman and board him." An
exact statement of the annual income from forest, field, land,
wood, meadows, cattle etc. and a report about the well that
was built at the rectory in 1600 closes his report.

Out of his book *Gravamina* about the observance of the
Sundays, the description of the habits at that time is remarkable, f. i. "that the young people carry cheese and bread to
the fields at Whitsuntide and have all sorts of entertainment
there, and that the young people come into the village in the
morning of the Peter and James' day, shouting loudly, on
horseback, and that they ride three times around the lime tree
with a boy enveloped in twigs and branches which super-
stitious people tear off, as these are said to be good against
evils." Furthermore, Hoffius mentions how the boys beg for
eggs on Shrove-Tuesday and "run around with different par-
ties and disdain the word of God," also people who apparently
cure cattle by magic and do other miraculous things, such as
Scherhans of Gimbweiler, Alexander, flayer of Walhausen and
Henrich, shepherd of Wolfersweiler "who are much run after
and are therefore suspected of fortune-telling and conjuring."
The very detailed list of the clergymen's salaries, sheet 118-
121, by the clergyman Johannes Helffenstein of Konken is
likewise important for the history of that place. He refers to
an older scheme — dated April 18th, 1589 — which contains
apart from the numerous fields, meadows and land with their
old names and their neighbors, the names of the seven jurymen and censors of Konken at that time (1589), i. e. Johann
Keller of Concken, Nickel Jung of Albsen, Mattheis Nickel of
Selchenbach, Seimet Kein [1] of Herschweiler, Johann Morgenstern of Langenbach, Velten of Pfedersheim and Clossmann
Hanns of Croftelbach.

HERM. FRIEDR. MACCO.

BERLIN—STEGLITZ, January 18th, 1927.

---

[1] In the copy (1609) probably written incorrectly instead of Klein,
see f. 127.

PROTESTANT CHURCH ARCHIVES OF KONKEN, NEAR KUSEL.

No. 41½ Parochial Visitations, 1609.

Folio Volume, Without Cover, Original.

fol. 2	List of the annual competency and the parish properties of the parish *Alten Glan.*
fol. 6	37 hearths or houses were in Alten Glan anno 1609, in the week post cantate.
Peasant and "reysiger im ausschuss"	1. Thomas *Kalckbrenner*, Margret his wife, have 2 sons, one daughter, 1 male servant, 1 female servant.
Farmer and day-labourer	2. Simon *Zimmer* and Engel have 1 daughter and the husband's mother, a widow, 78 years old.
Bell-ringer	3. Peter *Aulenbacher*, Margret, have 3 daughters, 1 son.
The tailor, innkeeper, publican and censor	4. Hanns *Theobaldt*, Margret have 1 son, eleven years old, and in their house lives their daughter Catharin and Johannes, her husband, who do not have any children.
The shepherd	5. Daniel and Gertrud have 3 sons and 1 daughter.
	6. Margret *Schmiddin*, widow, 1 son, 1 daughter.
	7. *Reuttersch* Clärgen, widow.
A baker	8. Peter Rautth, Elisabeth, have only 1 daughter who married the bell-ringer, No. 3.
Peasant	9. Nohe *Becker*, Margret, have 2 sons, 3 daughters.
Tailor	10. Johannes *Peter*, Margret, 1 son, 12 years old, 3 daughters.
	11. *Pettges* Engel, widow, has one female servant.
Peasant	12. Peter Timmer, Maria, have 2 sons, 1 daughter.
Linen-weaver	13. Veltin Weber, Margret, 1 daughter, 12 years old, 1 son, 3 years old.
Farmer and butcher	14. Anthes *Reutter*, Agnes, 3 sons, 2 daughters.
Linen-weaver and farmer	15. *Veltins* Hans, Martha, have 2 sons, one of them 11 years, the other 7 years old, 1 daughter.
Farmer	16. Jonas *Becker*, Catharin, 1 son, 13 years old, 1 daughter, 9 years old.
Farmer	17. Hanns *Schuck*, Agnes, have in their house the old Jonas, his brother-in-law, 2 sons, 1 daughter.
Farmer	18. Peter Klein, Barbel, 2 sons, 1 daughter.
Farmer and shearer	19. Adam *Scherer*, Ketter.
Farmer	20. Hans Weber, Eva, 2 sons, 1 daughter.
Clergyman	21. Johannes Foenilius, Kunigund, have three daughters of his first wife.

Vine-dresser and butcher	22. *Elsen* Hanns, Engel, have in their house 2 sons, 4 daughters.
Shoemaker	23. Nickel Sawr, Engel, 1 daughter.
Farmer	24. Johannes *Jung*, Agnes, have one son.
Farmer	25. Anthes *Dick*, Barbel, 5 sons, 2 daughters, children and step-children, and 1 male servant.
Farmer	26. Michael *Jöckel, Catharin*, have 1 son.
Carpenter	27. David *Jöckel*, Eva, have no child.
Carpenter	28. Hanns *Zimmerman*, Margret, 1 daughter of 13 years, 1 son 10 years old,—have in their house their son-in-law and his wife Agnes with one daughter.
Linen-weaver Farmer	29. Johannes *Bahl*, Margret, have in their house *Haman* their son-in-law, Marei their daughter, with one son and one daughter.
Farmer	30. Johann *Kleinmann*, Mari, have a son, 10 years old.
Vine-dresser	31. *Zimmer* Daniel, Catharina, 1 daughter, 10 years old.
Carpenter	32. Hanns *Schneider*, widower, has in his house a son-in-law.
Carpenter	Nickel *Zimmermann*, Margret, who have 3 daughters, 1 male servant and one female servant.
Farmer	33. Johannes *Zimmer*, Margret, 3 sons, 3 daughters, have Cläusgen, his father, a widower, in their house.
Vine-dresser	34. Abraham *Lorentz*, Martha, one female servant.
Farmer	35. Daniel *Kock*, Els,* [his wife] have one son, twenty years old.
Farmer	36. Daniel *Bub*, Els, 4 sons, 1 daughter.
Carpenter	37. Reinhard *Zimmerman*, Maria, 1 son, 2 daughters, 1 male servant.

Thus, at the above time there were in Alten Glan 46 married couples, i. e. 46 husbands and 46 wives, also 3 widowers and 4 widows, 47 sons and 45 daughters, item 5 male servants, 4 female servants, summarum 200 persons in Alten Glan.

f. 7. v.   There are 16 hearths or houses in *Pattersbach*, anno 1609, in the week post Cantate.

1. Daniel *Martin*, farmer, Maria, 5 sons, 1 daughter.
2. Johann *Dipurger*, farmer, Maria, 1 son, 3 daughters.
3. Johannes *Zimmerman*, carpenter and day-labourer, Ketter, 3 sons.
4. *Schneiders* Hanns, censor and butcher, Maria, whose children are married, have 2 servant-boys.
5. Abraham *Schneider*, tailor, Sara, 2 sons, 2 daughters.
6. Johannes *Becker*, vine-dresser and day-labourer, Clara, 2 sons, 1 daughter.
7. Johann *Thomae*, farmer, Engel, 2 sons and Liesse, his mother, a widow.
8. Jacob *Schaafhirt*, shepherd, Appel, 1 son, 3 daughters, 1 male servant.

---

* An abbreviation for Elizabeth.

9. Abraham *Weber*, linen-weaver, Liesa, 2 daughters, one of them being 22 years old, the other 5 years old.

10. *Schneider* Abram, vine-dresser, Marj, whose children are married, have one female servant.

11. *Thomas* Martin, vine-dresser, Margret, one female servant.

12. Jeremias *Metzler*, linen-weaver and butcher, 1 son, 2 daughters, 1 male servant.

13. Gerhard *Sneider*, vine-dresser, Maria, 1 son, 9 years old, have Götz, his mother, a widow, in their house.

14. Johannes *Offerbacher*, the cowherd, Appel, 2 sons, 1 daughter.

15. Johannes *Friderich*, peasant and vine-dresser, Margret, 3 daughters, the eldest being 10 years old, have Barbel, her mother, a widow, in their house.

16. Samuel *Müller*, miller, Margret, three daughters, three sons and one miller's servant, have in their house Catharin, their eldest daughter with her husband Johannes and Born Hanns, her father, a widower.

fol. 8	In *Bettesbach* there are 11 Hearths or houses anno 1609 in the week post Cantate.
Linen-weaver	1. Abraham *Herttel*, Engel his wife, have 3 sons and 4 daughters.
Vine-dresser	2. Seimet *Bawr*, Liesa, have 2 daughters.
Shoemaker	3. Wendel *Sawr*, Margret, have 3 sons, 1 daughter.
	4. *Weber* Ketter, a widow, 1 female servant.
Vine-dresser and farmer	5. Johann *Christmann*, Sara, have 1 son, 1 daughter.
ditto	6. Nickel *Schwodt*, Els,* have 3 sons, 1 daughter.
Censor, assistant "Reysiger im Ausschuss"	7. Hanns *Ulrich*, Eva, have 3 sons, 2 daughters.
Farmer	8. Johannes *Alt*, Sara, have 1 son, 1 daughter.
Blacksmith	9. Daniel *Schmidt*, Margret, have 2 daughters.
Thatcher	10. *Seimet* and Maria have 1 daughter.
Shepherd	11. Hans *Schääfer*, Sönngen, have no children.
fol. 8 v.	At *Soltzbach* there are 6 hearths or houses anno 1609 in the week post Cantate.
Vine-dresser	1. Johannes *Jost*, Els,* have 2 sons, 2 daughters.
Linen-weaver and church Jurat	2. Hanns *Gerhard*, Ketter, have from their former marriages his son Johannes, Linen-weaver and farmer, and her daugher Ketter who is married and has 1 son, 1 daughter and 1 male servant, in their house.
Farmer	3. Nickel *Rudt*, Engel, have 3 sons, the eldest of whom is nine years old, 2 daughters.
Cowherd	4. Jost *Hirtt*, Barbel, have children who are married.

* Probably an abbreviation for Elizabeth.

Farmer	5. Johannes *Peil,* Catharin, 2 sons, 1 daughter, and Appel, her mother, a widow.
Farmer	6. Johannes *Hoffmann,* Anna, have 4 sons, 2 daughters and Klein Ketter, a widow, 80 years old.
fol. 9	At *Friedelhausen* there are ten hearths or houses anno 1609 in the week post Cantate.
Censor and justiciary	1. Abraham *Krehmer* and Elsa, have 1 son, 1 daughter.
Farmer	2. Veltin *Doll,* a widower, 2 sons, 3 daughters.
Farmer	3. Johannes *Weber,* Kunigund, have no child yet.
Day-labourer, stone-cutter, whitewasher	4. Heyrich (name missing) (married couple) 2 sons, have in their house Christof Bauldot, Barbel, married couple.
Brick-layer	5. Hanns *Wolff,* Marj, have 1 son, 1 daughter his step-children.
Vine-dresser	6. Daniel *Kremer,* Amelej, have 2 daughters.
Farmer	7. Joes *Kremer,* Götz, 1 daughter, 1 son, Els, his mother, a widow.
Farmer	8. Theobald *Glan,* Catharin, 1 son, 1 daughter.
Farmer	9. *Heyrichs* Michel, Els have 3 daughters.
Cowherd	10. *Friederich,* Margreth, have 3 sons.

fol. 12.

A List of all inhabitants of the parish, husbands, wives, sons, daughters, male servants and female servants in the parish *Flürscappeln* has been written down by me, Johannen Sibelium, clergyman, anno 1609, on the 8th day of May.

The parish church is at Flürscappeln and the following villages belong to same:

1. Gumbsweiler   3. Pielsbach ⎫
2. Welchweiler   3. Ulmet   ⎬ are one borough
                                                  ⎭
4. Ertesbach   6. Irtzweiler
5. Oberalben   6. Huffersweiler
7. Ratsweiler and Brucken are one borough

Nr. 5   *Flürscappeln,* consisting of 3 hearths or houses.

Clergyman: Johannes *Sibelius,* Maria his wife, have 3 sons, 2 daughters, 1 female servant.

Mayor and "Kirchenschaffner" [churchwarden] Abraham *Preuel,* Engel his wife, have 2 sons, 1 daughter, a boy or servant, 2 female servants.

Pistor: Nickel *Becker,* Margreta his wife, have 4 sons, 3 daughters.

f. 12 v.   *Ulmet.*

Vietor 1. Peter *Küffer,* Eva his wife, have 3 sons.
2. Adam *Cuntz,* Barbara his wife, have a female servant.
3. Hans *Pohtt,* Elisabeth his wife, have 1 son, 2 daughters.

Sartor

4. Hans *Klein,* Elisabeth his wife, have one female servant.

Sutor and church Jurat

5. Jacob *Klein,* Margretha his wife, have 1 son, 1 female servant.

6. Andreas *Sprenck,* Eva his wife, have 2 sons, 1 daughter, 1 male servant, 1 female servant.

7. Johannes *New,* Margretha his wife, have 2 sons, 2 daughters, 2 male servants, 1 female servant.

8. Johannes *Carius,* Catharina his wife, have no children and no servants.

Lapicida

9. Nickel, *Naw,* Maria, his wife, have 1 son.

Faber ferrarius

10. Bast Fyck, Anna his wife.

Coriarius

11. Johannes *Lauer,* Elisabeth his wife.

Lanius

12. Jonas *Büttel,* Catharina his wife, have 2 sons, 3 daughters.

13. Johannes *Buttel,* Engel his wife, have 1 female servant.

14. Theobald *Bauer,* Eva his wife, have 1 son, 1 female servant.

15. Abraham *Schreiner,* Geza his wife, have 1 male servant, 2 female servants.

Scabinus

16. Jacob *Drum,* Engel his wife, have 3 sons, 1 female servant.

Sutor

17. Abraham *Drum,* Eva his wife, have 3 sons, 1 daughter, 1 female servant.

f. 13 Sutor

18. Johannes *Küffer,* Catharina his wife, have 1 daughter, 1 female servant.

19. Hans *Pfeiffer,* Margreta his wife.

20. Abraham *Schwad,* Engel his wife.

Lanius

21. Hans *Gross,* Catharina his wife, have 1 daughter.

22. Matthes Köll, Margreta his wife, have 2 sons, 1 daughter.

23. Johannes *Schafhirt,* Barbara his wife, have 1 son, 1 daughter, 1 male servant.

24. Johannes *Kühehirt,* Catharina his wife, have 1 male servant.

Sutor

25. Abraham *Wagner,* Eva his wife, have 1 daughter, 2 sons, 1 male servant.

Faber ferrarius

26. Johannes *Schmidt,* Margreta his wife, have 2 sons, 2 daughters.

Faber ferrarius

27. Nickel *Schreiner,* Sara his wife, have 3 sons, 1 daughter.

28. Jonas *Becker,* Margreta his wife, have 1 daughter.

Lanius

29. Anthes *Schwob,* Agnes his wife, have 4 sons, 2 daughters.

30. Johannes *Kalckbrenner,* Margreta his wife, have 2 sons, 1 daughter.

Vidui et viduae in Ulmet and Pielsbach.

1. Johannes *Carius.*   2. Balthasar *Kuffer.*
3. Willibert has 1 son, 1 daughter.
4. Elisabeth, Hans *Pott's* widow.
5. Martha, Johannes *Blutten's* widow, has 1 son, 2 daughters.

fol. 13 v.   *Pielsbach.*

Censor, faber   1. Peter Fyckeysen, Eva his wife, have 3 sons, 1 daugh-
armamentarius   ter, 1 male servant, 1 female servant.
Lanius   2. Hans *Koch,* Catharin his wife, have 4 sons, 2 daugh-
                   ters.
Pistor   3. Abraham *Becker,* Esther his wife, have 3 sons, 2
                   daughters.
                4. Hans *Thomae,* Margreta his wife.
Caupo   5. Johannes *Schreiner,* Margret his wife, have 1 son, 1
                   daughter.
Sartor   6. Johannes *Kayss* (formerly Kaniss), Magdalena his
                   wife, 1 son, 2 daughters.
                7. Nickel *Naw,* Sara his wife, have 1 son.
                8. Jeremias *Petri,* Engel his wife, have 3 sons, 1 daugh-
                   ter.
                9. Reinhard *Stroschnitter,* Eva his wife, have 1 son, 2
                   daughters.
               10. Christman *Naw,* Barbara his wife.
               11. Daniel *Cappel,* Susanna his wife, have 2 sons, 2
                   daughters.
Sartor   12. Johannes *Leim,* Maria his wife, have 1 son, 1 daugh-
                   ter.
               13. Adam *Flesch,* Engel his wife, have 1 son.
               14. Georgius *Stricker,* Appolonia his wife.
               15. Adam *Cappel,* Eva his wife, have 3 sons, 2 daughters.
Church Jurat   16. Johannes *Schwab,* Catharina his wife, have 1 son, 1
                   daughter, 1 male servant.
               17. Nickel *Weissgerber,* Margret his wife, have 1 son, 3
                   daughters.
Pistor   18. Johannes *Recker,* Engel his wife, have 2 sons, 1 male
                   servant, 1 female servant.
Coriarius   19. Johannes *Ruht,* Appolonia his wife.

                        Ertesbach.

                1. Hans *Herman,* Maria his wife, have 3 sons, 1 female
                   serv.
                2. Jonas *Kramp,* Maria his wife, have 2 sons, 2 daugh-
                   ters, 1 female servant.
Scabinus   3. Nickel *Herman* est viduus, has one female servant.
Lanius   4. Hans *Mack,* Catharina his wife, have 1 son, 1 daugh-
                   ter.
                5. Abraham *Jung,* Martha his wife, have 1 son, 1
                   daughter.
                6. David *Mack,* Eva his wife, have 1 son, 1 daughter.

7. Abraham *Mack*, Barbara his wife, have 3 sons, 2 daughters.
8. Philip *Weber*, Barbara his wife, have 1 son, 1 daughter.
9. Theobald *Heysel*, Anna his wife, have 1 son, 1 fem. servant.
10. Johannes *Heysel*, Catharina his wife, have 2 sons, 1 female servant.
11. Johannes *Baur*, Maria his wife, have 2 sons, 2 daughters, 1 female servant.
12. Johannes *Schmid*, Esther his wife, have 1 son.
13. Adam *Gerhard*, Barbara his wife, have 3 sons, 1 daughter.

Church Jurat

14. Abraham *New*, Sara his wife, have one of their sons-in-law in their house:

Lanius

Johannes Becker, Engel his wife, have 3 sons, 2 daughters.
15. Johannes *Heysel*, Margreta his wife, have 1 daughter, 1 male servant, 1 female servant.

Sutor

16. Daniel *Dick*, Elisabeth his wife, have 1 daughter, 1 male servant.
17. Adam *Beyer*, cujus conjux lepra correpta jam in xenodochio Bipontino commoratur, have 2 sons, 1 female servant.

Lanius

18. Jacob *Scheid*, Margreta his wife, have 3 sons, 3 daughters.
19. Samuel *Dick*, Margreta his wife, have 1 son, 1 daughter.

Faber
ferrarius

20. Jacob *Alt*, Catharina his wife, have 2 sons.
21. Johannes *Dick*, Elisabeth his wife, have 1 son, 1 daughter, 1 female servant.

Sartor et
Censor

22. Daniel *Schneider*, Catharina his wife, have 1 fem. servant.

Sutor

23. Johannes *Jung*, Gertrud his wife, have 1 son, 1 daughter, 1 male servant.
24. Wolf *Friderich*, the shepherd, Margreta his wife, have 1 son, 1 daughter, 1 male servant.
25. Johannes *Dick*, Catharina his wife, have 2 sons, 1 daughter.
26. Johannes *Becker*, Maria his wife, have 1 daughter, 1 female servant.

Unica vidua Margreta, *Steinhausen* selig relicta vidua.

fol. 15

Oberalben.

1. Antes *Welsch*, Catharina his wife, 1 son, 1 daughter.
2. Johannes *Flesch*, Elisabeth his wife, 3 sons, 4 daughters.
3. Cunrad *David*, Margreta his wife, 1 son, 3 daughters, 1 male servant.

4. Jacob *Bub*, Margreta his wife, 1 male servant.
5. Johannes the *shepherd*, Cunigund his wife, 1 son, 2 daughters.
6. Abraham *Mack*, Catharina his wife.
7. Claus *Knab*, Margreta his wife, 2 daughters.
8. Jacob *Jung*, Susanna his wife, 1 son.
9. Nickel *Mohr*, Barbara his wife.
10. Johannes *Muller*, Elisabeth his wife, 1 son, 1 daughter, 1 male servant.

Censor
11. Hans *Müller*, Dorothea his wife, 1 son, 2 daughters.
12. Nickel *Gaw*, Elisabeth his wife, 1 son, 1 daughter.
13. *Emerich*, Margreta his wife, 1 son, 2 daughters.
Velten, a widower.

Ihrtzweiler and *Huffertsweiler* are one borough.

1. Hans *Weber*, Sara his wife.
2. Nickel *Queck*, Catharina his wife, 4 sons, 2 daughters.
3. Johannes *Queck*, Appolonia his wife, 2 sons, 2 daughters.

Censor
4. Abraham *Lork*, Catharina his wife, 1 son, 1 daughter.
5. Johannes *Schafhirt*, Engel his wife, 3 sons, 3 daughters.
6. Johannes *Lorck*, Elizabeth his wife, 5 sons, 2 daugters.
7. Johannes *Drum* est viduus, has one female servant.
8. Johannes *Dol*, Margreta his wife, 3 sons, 3 daughters.
9. Jacob *Diel*, Maria his wife, 1 son, 3 daughters.
10. Peter *Köll*, Appolonia his wife, 3 sons, 3 daughters.
11. Michael *Kuhe*, Catharina his wife, 1 male servant.

fol. 16
Ratsweiler and *Brucken* are one borough.

1. Peter *Jung*, Maria his wife, 2 sons, 1 daughter, 1 male servant.
2. Peter *Hertel*, Margreta his wife, 2 sons, 1 female servant, have one of their married sons in their house, called Johannes, Engel his wife.

Pistor
Censor
3. Theobald *Becker*, Maria his wife, 1 female servant.
4. Hans *Herman*, Elisabeth his wife, 1 male servant, 1 fem. servant.
5. Johannes *Pohtt*, Appolonia his wife, 1 son, 1 female servant.
6. Hans *Born*, Margreta his wife, 2 sons, 2 male servants, 2 female servants.
7. Jacob *Keller*, Eva his wife, 1 son, 1 daughter.
They have a son-in-law in their house, Nickel *Steinmetz*, Margret his wife.
8. Abraham *Schuch*, Sara his wife, 2 sons, 3 daughters.
9. Johannes *Klein*, Catharina his wife, 2 sons, 2 daughters.
10. Johannes *Hanss*, Engel his wife, 2 sons, 3 daughters, 1 male servant, 1 female servant.

11. Hans *Meyer*, Eva his wife, 1 female servant.
12. Johannes *Schmidt*, Margreta his wife, 2 sons, 3 daughters.
13. Conrad *Coster*, Maria his wife, have a son who married Catharina, and has 3 children.
14. Johannes *Zimmerman*, Eva his wife, 1 son.
15. Johannes *Schuster*, conjugem, p.p. admissum adulterium repudiavit, has 1 son.
16. Johannes *Schafhirt*, Martha his wife, 1 son Christoffel, who is married, Catharina his wife.
17. Jacob *Schmidt*, Appolonia, 1 son, 2 daughters.

fol. 16 v.   *Welchweiler.*

Church Jurat
1. Abraham *Olien*, Sara his wife, 2 sons, 1 daughter.
2. Bast *Keyser*, Eva his wife, 1 son, 3 daughters.
3. Claus *Tauselbach*, Elisabeth his wife, 1 daughter, have in their house a son-in-law, Nickel *Schmid*, Anna his wife, 1 son, 3 daughters.
4. Michael *Oliger*, Maria his wife, 1 daughter.

Censor
5. Peter *Sorg*, Eulalia his wife, 2 sons, 2 daughters.
6. Eva *Freyin*, a widow, 1 son.
7. Simon *Sorg*, Catharina his wife, 2 sons, 2 daughters.
8. Peter *Felss*, Margret his wife, 1 son, 2 daughters.
9. German *Leinenweber*, Susanna his wife, 1 son, 2 daughters.
10. Catharina *Steyert*, a widow, 2 sons, 1 daughter.
11. Johannes *Peter*, Catharina his wife, 1 daughter.
12. Cunrad *Leinenweber*, Margret his wife, 1 son, 5 daughters.
13. Barbara, a widow, 1 daughter.
14. German *Clauss*, Elisabeth his wife, 2 sons, 2 daughters.
15. Johannes *Fischer*, Anna his wife, 2 daughters.
16. Bast *Felss*, Anna his wife, 3 sons.
17. Sara, a widow, 1 daughter.
18. Remig *Matthess*, Catharina his wife, 1 son, 1 daughter.
19. Nickel *Ruht*, Appolonia his wife, 1 son, 1 daughter.
20. *Anthess* Heinrich, Margretha his wife, 3 daughters.
21. Michael *Mohr*, Agnes his wife, 1 daughter, 1 male servant.
22. Hans *Schafhirt*, Elisabeth his wife, 4 sons, 2 daughters.

fol. 17   *Gumbsweiler*, is a "filial".

Censor
1. Michael *Schmidt*, Catharina his wife, 1 son, 1 fem. servant.
2. Hans *Georg*, Elisabeth his wife, 1 son.
3. Catharina, Hans *Felsen's* left widow, 1 son and 1 son-in-law: Hans *Cusseller*, Lucia his wife.

4. Thomas *Scherer*, Anna his wife, 1 daughter, 1 male servant, 1 female servant.
5. Thomas *Kolb*, viduus, has a married son in his house, Hans *Kolb*, Catharina his wife, 1 daughter, 1 male servant.
6. Abraham *Kolb*, Margreta his wife, 1 son, 3 daughters.
7. Gerloch *Schwab*, Elisabeth his wife, 2 sons, 3 daugters.
8. Nickel *New*, Elisabeth his wife, 1 female servant.
9. Wendel *Felss*, Agnes his wife, 5 sons, 1 daughter.
10. Hans *Schnach*, Margret his wife, 2 daughters, 1 male servant.
11. Noa *Becker*, Lucia his wife, 3 sons.
12. Johannes *Schumacher*, Barbara his wife, 2 sons, 1 male servant.
13. Wendel *Schmidt*, Catharina his wife, 1 son.
14. Geza, vidua, 2 sons, 1 daughter.
15. Jacob *Hübsch*, Anna his wife, 1 daughter.
16. Abraham *New*, Margretha his wife, 1 son, 1 daughter.
17. Thomas *Wentz*, Barbara his wife, 1 daughter, 1 male servant; has in his house a mother-in-law, called Barbara.

f. 24, No. 8   *Hintzweiler* [1] has 20 hearths.

1. Antonius *Beiel*, Catarina uxor, Tilemanns filius, is married, conjux (ejus) filia Maria, nepos Elisabeth.
2. Johannes *Gerpacher*, Eva ux., Jacob, Peter, Johannes filii, Catharina, Margreta, Anna, Maria, Barbara filiae.
3. *Peter* Jacob, Maria Salome ux., Maria filia, Sebastian servus, Elisabeth, vidua, is in the house of this Petro, her son.

Agricolae

4. Joannes *Cratz*, Margreta ux., Joannes *Ödinger* gener eadem domo, Catharina conjux. Barbara (Cratz) filia inupta.
5. Johannes *Gross*, Catharina ux., Sebastianus *Scherer*, adoptivus et conjux Gertrud, Johannes nepos, Jacob servus.
6. Sebastian *Weiss*, Margreta ux., Sebastian, married, Johannes, filii, Maria filia, Sebastian servus.
7. Abraham *Gerbacher*, Sara ux., Sara, ancilla.
8. Joannes *Clein*, Maria ux., Jacob, filius coelebs, Joannes, nepos, Appollonia, ancilla.

Textor   9. Jonas *Petri*, Maria ux., Daniel et Antonius, filii, Catharina filia, Jacob servus.

Vietor   10. Herman *Bartz*, Maria ux., Joannes, Abraham filii, Catharina, Elisabeth, filiae.

Pistor   11. Daniel *Weiss*, Engel ux., Daniel, Joannes, Jacob, filii, Catharina, filia, Elisabeth, ancilla.

---

[1] In the valley of Essweiler.

Scrivarius	12. Johan *Seitz*, Elisabeth ux., Johan, Javob, Philipp, Abraham, Jeremias, filii, Maria, Margreta, filiae.
Faber	13. Joannes *Cratz*, Getza ux., Joannes, servus, Appolonia, ancilla.
Sartor	14. Joannes *Schmit*, Catharina ux., Abraham, Jeremias, filii, Joannes servus. Sebastian *Dönges*, lives with them, in the house of his son-in-law.
Textor	15. Peter *Schmit*, Maria ux.
Sutor	16. Abraham *Becker*, Margreta ux., Joannes, Sebastian, filii Margreta filiae, Catharina Hans, servus.

17. Noha *Schuch*, Margreta ux., Sebastian, Joannes, filii, Margreta filia.
18. Abraham *Pott*, Maria ux., Antonius, Sebastian filii, Catharina filia, Gertraud, vidua lives in the house of this Abraham, genero.

Mercenarii

19. Elias *Preuel*, Catharina ux., Anna Catharina et Margret filiae.
20. Sebastian *Tönges*, Maria ux., Margreta filia.

f. 24 v.   *Oberweiler* has 34 hearths.

Scabinus
Censor et
juratus

1. Joannes *Diel*, Verina ux., Carolus serv., Elisabeth anc.
2. Meinhard *Preud*, Margreta ux., Abraham fil., is married, conj. Magdalena, David nepos.
3. Peter *Gerpacher*, Barbara ux., Joannes, Sebastian filii, Maria, Magdalena, Elisabeth, Catharina filiae, Margreta ancilla.
4. Sebastian *Wolff*, Maria ux., Hans fil., Maria ancilla.
5. Hans *Cratz*, Engel ux., Jacob, married, Catharina conjux, Catharina et Barbara nepotes.
6. Elias *Hensel*, Engel ux., Margareta, Maria, Catarina, filiae. Elisabeth vidua, Elias' mother, lives in his house.
7. Theobalt *Riemenschneider*, Magdalena ux., Margreta, Anna Catharina filiae.

Agricolae

8. Peter *Laufferweiler*, Catharina ux., Catharina ancilla.
9. Peter *Hausweiler*, Elisabeth ux., Sebastian fil., Barbara, Margreta, Maria, Martha filiae.
10. Georg *Vetter*, Elisabeth ux., Sebastian filius, married, conjux called Maria. Johannes servus.
11. Johannes *Wollenschläger*, Catharina ux., Margreta ancilla.
12. Joannes *Clintz(in)g(er)*, Catharina ux., Joannes, Abraham, Hans filii, Elisabeth et Catharein filiae.
13. Joannes *Doll*, Magdalena ux., Meinhart, Abraham, Hans filii, Barbel et Engel filiae, Appolonia ancilla.
14. Abraham *Diel*, Elisabeth ux., Jacob, Elias, Sebastian filii, Margreta, Anna, Elisabeth, Martha filiae.

Textores

15. Jacob *Wöber*, Margreta ux., Sebastian filius.
16. Elias *Wollenschläger*, Martha ux., Johannes fil. Catharina, Marei filiae.

Scabinus at Eisenbach	17. Jacob *Wolff*, Catharina uxor.
	fol. 25 v.
Lapicida	18. Johannes *Schuch*, Margreta ux., Hans Jacob et Hans Merten filii.
Fabri lignarii	19. Joannes *Zimmerman*, Catharina ux., Johannes filius, Catharina filia.
	20. Joan *Zimmerman*, Odilia ux., Jacob fil., Margreta filia.
Victores	21. Daniel *Schmit*, Margreta ux., Elias filius, Verina filia.
	22. Johan *Haas*, Margreta ux.
Mercenarii	23. Reichart *Hanseman*, Barbara ux., Joannes fil. Maria filia.
	24 Georg *Remheimer*, Catharina ux., Marei filia.
	25. Samuel *Vetter*, Margreta ux., Johan, Abraham filii, Catharina, Verina filiae.
	26. Georg *Weiss*, Catharina ux., Margreta filia.
	27. Theobalt *Hammell*, Margreta ux., Daniel, Samuel filii.
	28. Joanes *Eckel*, Eva ux., Elisabeth, Catharina filiae.
	29. Philippus *Prewell*, Catharina ux., Johannes filius.
Mendicus	30. Peter *Censs*, Sara ux.
	31. Margreta, *Hauh* Hansen's widow, Catharina, ancilla.
	32. Catharina, *Spor* Hansen's widow, Agnes ancilla.
	33. Maria, *Vetter* wöbers' widow.
	34. Magdalena, *Schormanns* Hensen's widow.

Horspach [1] has 13 hearths.

Censor	1. Johan *Mohr*, Anna ux., Anna Catharina, Maria, Magdalena filiae, Niclas servus, Barbara famula, Peter Diel, viduus, senator etc.

2. Conrad des Gebharten filius, coelebs, Gebharth *Bindel*, viduus.

3. Tobias *Baum*, Anna Catharina ux., Joannes fil., Anna Maria, Margreta filiae, Johannes servus, Maria Elisabeth famula.

4. Daniel *Doll*, Catharina ux., Daniel fil., Margreta, Magdalena filiae.

5. Peter *Werner*, Elisabeth ux., Johan, Sebastian, Jacob filii, Margreta, Maria filiae.

6. Johan *Bender*, Agnes ux., Jacob, Hans filii.

7. Joseph *Diepurg*, Elisabeth ux., Johannes fil., Margreta Catharina, Anna, Engel, Maria, Elisabeth filiae.

8. Daniel *Diel*, Anna ux., Johan, Jacob, Hans filii, Margreta, Elisabeth filiae.

9. Johannes *Berg*, Martha ux., Verina filia.

10. Clos *Bauer*, Elisabeth ux., Peter, Johan, Hans filii, Catharina, Eva, Maria, filiae.

11. Johann *Werner*, Engel ux., Wendel fil. Maria filia, Engel famula.

---

[1] Now Horschbach near Hinzweiler, south of St. Julian.

12. Jacob *Diel,* Engel ux., Margretha famula.
13. Joannes *Diel,* Barbara ux., Noha, Tobias filius, Anna Maria, Elisabeth filiae.

27 v.
fol. $\overline{28}$ *Aspach* [1] has 17 houses.

Scabinus   1. Jacob *Wolf,* Catharina ux., Johannes married (with) Maria, Daniel (her child), Hans, servus, Elias filius, (Jacobi).

Censor   2. Abraham *Chuno,* Sara ux., Maria, Elisabeth, Barbara filiae, Johannes et Jacob servi, Gertraut famula.
3. Daniel *Bauer,* Elisabeth ux., Elias, Niclas, Daniel filii.
4. Clos *Chuno,* Maria ux., Jacob filius, Catharina, Elisabeth, Barbel filiae, Jacob servus.
5. Daniel *Bauer,* Catharina ux., Sara filia.

Agricolae   6. Joannes *Werner,* Catharina ux., Conrad, Niclas, Abraham, Michel, Jacob filii, Maria filia.
7. Daniel *Schaff,* Maria ux., Barbara, Catharina, Maria filiae.
8. Johan *Gauer,* Appolonia ux., Niclas filius, Maria filia.
9. Johan *Ruth,* Apollonia ux., Jacob, Abraham filii, Elisabeth, Catharina filiae.

10. Clos *Schuster,* Barbara ux., Joannes filius, Maria, Elisabeth filiae.
11. Hans *Spön,* Getza ux.
12. Elias *Poël,* Anna ux., Niclas, Daniel, Joannes filii.

Mercenarii   13. Stefan Wol, Elisabeth ux., Elias fil, Catharein, Elisabeth filiae.
14. Velten *Keller,* Justina ux., Anna famula.
15. Johan *Kessler,* Catharina ux., Michel filius.
16. Jacob *Kessler,* Catharina ux., Hans Jacob, Anthes filii.

17.   David, Abraham filii.[2]

The Leienberg is situated between Hinzweiler and Wolfstein.

28 v.
fol. $\overline{29}$ *Nartzweiler* has 19 houses.

Censor   1. Johan *Kessell,* Margretha conjux, Jacob filius, married, conjux ejus Anna, nepotes [4] Catharina, Daniel, Johannes, Jacob.
2. Joannes *Diel,* Appollonia conj. Elisabeth, lame, Johannes servus.

Agricolae   3. Johan *Pot,* Catharina conj., Jacob, Daniel, Johann, Hans filii, Martha, Anna filiae.
4. Daniel *Jung,* Engel conj., Jacob filius, Maria filia.

---

[1] Now Aschbach, east of Hinsweiler.

[2] As the place for the name of the parents is free, they seem to belong to ''Jacob Ley, viduus, conjux ob delicta in exilio'' and are his sons.

[3] Nerzweiler, north of Hinzweiler.

[4] i. e. grandchildren of Johann Kessel and sons of Jacob.

Agricolae

  5. Jacob *Wolschlager*, Maria conj., Johan, Daniel, Hans filii, Anna Catharina filiae, et cujus Jacobi mater vidua.

  6. Best *Krill*, Barbara conj., Margretha filia, (et) Jacob viduus lives 6 years with his son Besten.

  7. Jacob *Rub*, Catharina conj., Hans, Jacob filii, Elisabeth, Margretha filiae, Haman, servus, Margreta famula.

  8. Johan *Koch*, Ela conj., Elisabeth filia, Johannes servus.

Lanius

  9. Daniel *Beller*, Elisabeth conj., Johan, Hans filii, Otilia famula.

 10. Sebastian *Beck*, Maria conj.

 11. Johan *Fritz*, Anna conj., Hans Theobalt fil., Catharina filia.

 12. Theobalt *Wöf* [1] Catharina conj.

 13. Johan *Friderich*, Eva conj., Hans Jacob, Hans, Hans Nickel filii.

 14. Elias *Clein*, Margreta, conj., Jacob, Johannes filii.

 15. Antonius *Kremer*, Catharina conj., Johannes filius, Anna filia.

Scabinus

 16. Jacob *Clein*, Martha conj., Martha famula.

 17. Velten *Schleich*, Anna conj., Sara, Otilia, Catharin, Margreta, filiae.

 18. Martha, Johan *Lejen* widow, Catharina et Anna filiae.

 19. Engel, the widow of the lame *Besten*.

29 v.
Fol. 30

Hoof *Letzweiler* has 2 houses.

Scabinus

  1. Johannes *Schuch*, viduus, Abraham, Johannes, Hans, Daniel filii, Catharina, Elisabeth, Margreta, Martha filiae.

Agricola

  2. Jonas *Schuch*, filius hujus, Margreta conjux, Johannes, Michael, Hans, Niclas filii.

Kirch *Hirsau* [2] has 2 houses.

Mercenarius

  1. Johann *Pfaff*, Christina conjux.

  2. Doncel [3] *Filtz*, Margreta conjux, Johannes Hansgen filii.

Hundheim [4] has 15 houses.

Censor et juratus

  1. Nicolaus *Feng*, Gertraud ux., Niclas serv. Magdalena, famula.

---

[1] Abbreviated after a badly written "f".

[2] Church of Hirschau between St. Julian and Offenbach at the Glan.

[3] Or Doncet.

[4] South of Offenbach at the Gl.

Agricolae

2. Johannes *Feng*, Susanna ux., Jacob, Elias, Jeremias filii, Anna, Eva, Margreta, Catharina filiae.
3. Conrad *Bürtell*, Catharina ux., Conrad, Johannes, Hans Peter filii, Margreta, Anna filiae.
4. Niclas *Schneid(er)*, Kunigund, ux., Sebastian fil. is married, conj. cuj. Catharina, Hans, Jacob, Kunigund, Margreta nepotes, Niclas servus.
5. Niclas *Scherer*, Catharina ux., Catharina, Anna, Marta fil.
6. Jonas *Römer*, Margreta ux., Wendel, Hans, Jacob, Johannes filii, Susanna, Anna, Margreta filiae, Maria famula.

Praetor 7. Johannes *Franck*, Anna ux., Georg, Hans Jacob filii.

Scabinus 8. Noha *Schnit*, Catharina ux., Noha filius mente captus Barbel, famula.

Miles 9. Noha *Georg*, Gertraud ux., Hans Michel, Noha filii, Margreta filia.

Lapicidi 10. Johan *Keller*, Martha ux., Anna filia.

Molitor 11. Jacob *Gosselman*, Getza ux., Adam, Johannes, Zacharius filii, Catharina, Elisabeth, Anna, Agatha filiae.

Mercenarius 12. *Anstadt* Bernhard, Appollonia ux., Magdalena, Gertraud filiae.

Mercenarius 13. Peter *Bernhard*, Anna ux., Elias filius, Maria, Catharina, Anna filiae.

Mercenarius 14. Jacob *Helrigel*, Maria ux., Gallus, Niclas, Michel filii, Engel, Anna, Catharina, Margreta filiae.

15. Catharina vidua *Kellers* Hansen, Nickel, Gallus filii, Margreta filia.

f. 31 v. *Hachenbach* has 10 houses.

Censor

1. Jonas *Wolschlager*, Catharina ux., Johannes *Bollenbacher* gener, Johannes filius, Barbara filia.
2. Clos *Becker*, Maria ux., Hans, Johann, Daniel filii, Margreta, Martha, Catharina, Elisabeth, all marriageable.

Coriarius
Agricolae
Sartor

3. Johan *Filtz*, Elisabeth ux., Johannes, Peter, Christianus filii, Maria filia.
4. Hans *Hertell*, Verina ux., Johann, Zacharias filii, Marei, lame, Elisabeth filiae.
5. Johan *Schuch*, Martha ux., Johan Jacob filius, Barbara, Maria filiae.
6. Johan *Petri*, Magdalena ux., Jacob, Hans, Peter, Daniel filii, Apollonia filia.

Faber 7. Johan *Helrigel*, Barbara ux., Conrad servus.

Vietor 8. Johan *Staud*, Apollonia ux., Hans, Peter filii.

Mercenarii

9. Palmen *Kaul*, Barbara ux.
10. Johan *Leim*, Catharina ux., Peter, Antonius, Hans filii, all marriageable, Barbara, Martha, Maria filiae.

Summa 10 mariti, 10 conjuges, 19 filii, 14 filiae.

Nr. 9	List of the inhabitants of the parishes *Bosenbach* and
Bosenbach [1]	*Nider Staufenbach*, also the Chapel of *Essweiler*.
Sartor	1. Hans *Sechs*, Gertraud his wife, Johannes child.
Scabinus et censor	2. Peter *Büttel*, Barbara h.w.
Sartor	3. Hans *Sawer*, Margreta h.w.
Agricola	4. Peter *Sawer*, Engelharda h.w. 1 child, Johannes.
"	5. Antonius *Becker*, Catrina h.w. 4 children, Maria, Eva, Hans, Johannes.
Operarius	6. Cun *Scheid*, Sara h.w. 1 grandchild, Peter Faz.
Miles et negociator	7. Henrich *Holz*, Maria h.w., 4 children: Ilsebeth, Nickel, Simon, Herman.
Molitor et operarius	8. Conrad *Kisel*, Geza h.w.
Agricola	9. Peter Klein, Margreta h.w. 4 children: Ilsebeth, Anna, Margreta, Hans.
Agricola	10. Johannes *Haisel*, Maria h.w. 3 children: Maria, Jacob, Anna.
Propola	11. Johannes *Sechs*, Margreta h.w.
Lapicida	12. Simon *Wil*, Margreta h.w., 1 child: Catrina.
Praetor et scabinus	13. Simon *Jung*, Gertraud h.w. 5 children: Johannes, Hans, Catrina, Maria Magdalena, Anna, Catrina.
Agricola	14. Hans *Specht*, Sinna.
Operarius	15. Thebald *Martin*, Anna, 6 children: Ilsebeth, Hans, Daniel, Catrina, Barbara, Margrete.
Agricola	16. Hans *Klinz*, Barbara, 1 son: Elias.
"	17. Daniel *Klinz*, Maria, 2 children: Catrina, Daniel.
Lanius et sartor	18. Dol *Koch*, Sara, 3 children: Ilsebeth, Daniel, Johannes.
Sartor et agricola	19. Jacob *Räib*, Margreta.
Agricola	20. Johannes *Thomas*, Marta.
Scabinus et censor	21. Nickel *Donzweiler*, Barbara.
fol. 40 v.	
Agricola	22. Daniel *Wenz*, Margreta, 4 children: Jacob, Catrina, Sara, Ilsebeth.
Scabinus et censor	23. Johannes *Staud* d(er) elter (the elder) Catrina, 4 children: Johannes, Hans, Margreta, Nickel.
Ovium pastor	24. Georg *Schafhirt*, Barbara, 2 children: Wendelin, Johannes.
Faber ferrarius	25. Hans *Schmit*, Sinna, 3 children: Hans, Marcus, Christoffel.
Agricola	26. Johannes Staud der Jünger (the younger), Maria, 3 children: Catrina, Simon, Anna.
Agricola	27. Velten *Thomas*, Ilsebeth, 1 son, Hans.
"	28. Stoffel *Theis*, Catrina.

---

[1] In the scheme parents and children are separated (two lists).

Operarius	29. Jacob *Elkel*, Ilsebeth, 4 children: Hans Henrich, Hans Jacob, Ilsebeth, Anna.
Agricola	30. Daniel *Büttel*, Anna, 5 children: Eva, Johannes, Margreta, Catrina, Johannes.
Lapicida	31. Hans *Wil*, Anna, 3 children: Martha, Johannes, Catrina.
Operarius	32. Hans *Kisel*, Barbara, 1 child: Johannes.
Lanificus	33. Peter *Schicht*, Barbara, 2 children: Catrina, Otilia.
Bubulcus	34. Jacob *Kühirt*, Margreta, 4 children: Anna Maria, Best, Hans Daniel, Hans Remig.
Agricola	35. Hans *Peter*, Ilsebeth, 8 children: Johannes, Daniel, Anna, Maria, Abraham, Ilsebeth, Hans, Jonas.
Censor et scabinus	36. Conrad *Büttel*, Margreta.
Operarius	Hans *Thebald*, widower.
	Margreta *Sechsin* ⎱ widows. Appollonia *Sechsin* ⎰
Male servants:	The clergyman's servant: Matthias *Dol.* The mayor's servant: Hans *Wirt.* Hans *Klinzen* boy: Best. Johannes *Stauden* des Jungen servant: Abraham *Thebald.* Hans *Willen* servant: Conrad *Leich.* Peter *Schicht's* apprentice: Balthasar.
Female servants.	The clergyman's maid: Engel *Müllers.* Peter *Büttel's* maid: *Niliesen* Ilse. Hans *Specht's* maid: Catrina. Nickel *Donzweiler's* maid: Appolonia.

fol. 41	*Nider Stauffenbach*
Scabinus et censor	1. Jonas Trein, Sara, 5 children: Ilsebeth, Daniel, Maria, Margreta, Catrina.
Agricola	2. Nickel *Bender*, Geza, 2 children: Thebald, Johannes.
Lapicida	3. Claus *Hirt*, Ilsebeth, 3 children: Hans, Johannes, Johas.
Lapicida	4. Jonas Stahl, Margreta, 3 children: Jacob, Sara, Jonas.
Operarius	5. Jacob *Emerich*, Ilsebeth.
Sartor	6. Nickel *Schneider*, Margreta, 3 children: Stephan, Gerhard, Nickel.
Pastor	7. Friedrich *Schafhirt*, Maria, 3 children: Michel, Hans, Claus.
Agricola	8. Joseph *Jung*, Barbara, 2 children: Johannes, Daniel.
Agricola et textor	9. Hans *Weber*, Margreta, 3 children: Johannes, Hans, Jacob.
Agricola	10. Claus *Loch*, Maria, 1 child: Jonas.
Sutor, lanius et agricola	11. Hans *Schumacher*, Catrina, 5 children: Simon, Barbara, Catrina, Jacob, Johannes.
	12. Sinna, the old *Schorer's* widow.
Male servant:	Jacob *Rostauscher*, the cowherd of the parish.
Female servant:	Nickel *Bender's* maid Sara.

fol. 41 a.   *Essweiler.*[1]

Agricola   1. Nickel *Reinheimer*, Catrina, 4 children: Hans, Lenhart, Wendel, Värein.

Agricola
et sartor   2. Hans *Baier*, Clara, 1 son: Hans.

Agricola   3. Jacob *Krämer*, Catrina, 5 children: Hans, Maria, Margreta, Johannes, Catrina.

Agricola   4. Hans *Herborn*, Magdalena.

Operarius   5. Hans *Snach*,[2] Engelhard (!), 1 child: Catrina.

Agricola   6. Johannes *Creuz*, Catrina.

Agricola
et censor   7. Daniel *Creuz*, Catrina.

Agricola   8. Hans *Creuz*, Engelhard, 2 children: Johannes, Catrina.
                 9. Daniel *Wirt*, Anna, 2 children: Margreta, Catrina.

Bubulcus   10. Jacob *Müller*, Engelhard.

Pastor ovium   11. Johannes *Schreiber*, Catrina, 6 children: Daniel, Matthias, Hans Daniel, Appollonia, Ilsebeth, Margreta.

Agricola   12. Hans *Vetter*, Catrina, 4 children: Jacob, Daniel, Sebastian, Samuel.

Operarius   13. Hans *Biel*, Ilsebeth, 2 children: Johannes, Daniel.

Figulus   14. Matthias *Hafener*, Appollonia, 1 son: Hans.

Agricola   15. Daniel *Hafener*, Ursula, 2 children: Catrina, Maria.

Faber ferrarius et
mechanicus   16. Hans *Schmit*, Martha, 6 children: Johannes, Maria, Hans, Daniel, Catrina, Jacob.

Agricolae   17. *Eckels* Best, Margreta, 1 child: Engelhard.
                18. Sebastian *Tiel*, Margreta, 4 children: Hans, Martha, Ilsebet, Johannes.
                19. Remig *Römer*, Johannes (!) (his wife).

Censor et
ptor nobilium   20. Jacob *Diez*, Maria, 4 children: Johannes, Antonius, Catrina, Eva.

Mercator   21. Johannes *Finck*, Cecilia, 5 children: Hans Jacob, Johannes, Elisabeth, Catrina, Theobald.

Agricola   22. Remig *Klein*, Engelhard, 2 children: Margreta, Daniel.

Faber ferrarius et
chirurgus   23. Daniel *Schmit*, Sara, 1 daughter: Catrina.

Sartor   24. Abraham *Schuch*, Margreta, 2 children: Johannes, Maria.

Agricolae   25. Joachim *Rump*, Catrina, 5 children: Daniel, Catrina, Hans, Antonius, Margreta.
                26. Lorenz *Klinz*, Catrina, 2 children: Peter, Margreta.
                27. Daniel *Klinz*, Catrina, 6 children: Daniel, Sara, Ilsebeth, Remig, Anna, Engelhard.

Operarius   28. Wendel *Schreiber*, Ilsebeth, 1 son: Hans.

Operarius   29. Jacob *Klinz*, Maria, 1 daughter: Maria Magdalena.

---

[1] Between Hinzweiler and Bosenbach.
[2] Fol 45 "Schnach".

Faber ferra- rius et praetor nobilis	30. Wendel *Schmit*, widower, 2 children: Daniel, Jacob.
	31. Ilsebeth, Johannes *Staben's* widow.[1]
	32. Ilsebeth, Abraham *Lochen's* widow.

Jacob, in Johannes *Creuz's* house.

Male servants { Johannes and Adam, in Daniel *Schmit's* house.

Hans in Ilsebeth's, Johannes *Staben's* widow's, house.

Eva, in Hans *Biel's* house.

Clara *Klinzin* in Remig *Römer's* house.

Female servants { Engel *Rumpin* in Jacob *Diez's* house.

Engel *Schormans*, in Daniel *Schmit's* house.

Ael in Abraham *Schuch's* house.

fol. 47/48   Inhabitants and houses of the churches of:

Baumholder.[2]

182 married couples, 14 [3] widowed people, 139 children, 34 servants and 82 hearths.

Ruebberg (Ruschberg).[4]

60 married couples, 5 widowed people, 68 children, 12 servants, 30 hearths.

Aulenbach.[5]

26 married couples, 1 widowed person, 42 children, 9 servants, 12 hearths.

Mambächel.[6]

56 married couples, 7 widowed people, 71 children, 12 servants, 28 hearths.

Grünenbach.[7]

28 married couples, 41 children, 5 servants, 13 hearths.

Rohnberg.[8]

26 married couples, 1 widowed person, 30 children, 4 servants, 11 fireplaces.

Fronhausen.[9]

26 married couples, 2 widowed people, 34 children, 7 servants, 12 hearths.

---

[1] Five children (fol. 46): Johannes, Jacob, Engel, Cetter, Margreta.

[2] North of Thal-Lichtenberg.

[3] Incorrect; there are 15. The children are not mentioned particularly.

[4] Ruschberg, north of Berschweiler.

[5] Northeast of Baumholder.

[6] Manbechel = Mambächel, north of Baumholder.

[7] Grünbach, northeast of Baumholder.

[8] Ronnenberg, east of Baumholder.

[9] Frohnhausen, north of Mambächel.

Denweyler, Fro(h)nbach.[1]

30 married couples, 3 widows, 33 children, 5 servants, 14 hearths.

Ertzweyler.[2]

8 married couples, 21 children, 2 servants, 8 hearths.

Langenbach.[3]

16 married couples, 2 widowed people, 19 children, 8 servants, 6 hearths.

fol. 47 Nr. 13 *Baumholder.*

1. Wilhelm *Eychorn*, mayor, Magdalena (Schultheiss).
2. Niclas *Brecher*, mayor, Margreta (Burgermeister).
3. Michel *Lohwer*, clerk of the court, Anna.
4. Johannes *Lutt*, bailiff, Otilia.

Court officials
5. Hensel *Weisgerber*, Eva.
6. *Josten* Peter, Catharina.
7. Laux *Kistenbacher*, Elsa.
8. Johannes *Disbes*, Agnes.
9. Ja(c)ob *Durr*, Catharina.
10. Niclas *Forster*, Barbara.

11. *Josten* Hans, censor, Gertrud.

Merchands and butchers
12. Johannes *Albinus*, schoolmaster, Catharina.
13. Paulus *Leffel*, Margreta.
14. Peter *Beschan*, Elisabeth.
15. Michel *Beschan*, Elisabeth.
16. Clos *Beschan*, Elisabeth.

Innkeeper ("Gasthalter")
17. Kais *Merten*, Catharina.
18. *Beschan* Hans, Maria.
19. Hans *Beschan*, Schönhen.

Linenweavers
20. *Claus*, Wilhelm, Elsa.
21. *Theus*, Catharina.
22. Clos *Thein*, Ermel.
23. *Johannes*, Maria.
24. Mattheus *Durr*, Engel.

Woolweavers
25. Haman *Weber*, Catharina.
26. Jacob *Gall*, Maria.

27. *Korner*, rope-maker, Elisabeth.

"Lohwer" (Tanners)
28. Johannes *Biel*, Eva.
29. Johannes *Hok*, Margreta.
30. Niclas *Hock*, Engel.

Shoemakers
31. Jacob, Elisabeth.
32. Michel *Bootz*, Anna.

Tailors
33. Antoin *Lower*, Catharina.
34. Andres *Kais*, Catharina.

Millers
35. Johannes, Walpurgis.
36. Johannes, Maria.
37. *Jost*, Maria.

---

[1] Dennweiler, Frohnbach, south of Baumholder.

[2] Erzweiler, east of Baumholder.

[3] Berglangenbach, south of Ruschberg and west of Baumholder.

Bricklayers	38. *Welsch*, Peter, Catharina.
	39. *Müller*, Cunrad, Catharina.
	40. *Gassen* Claus, Maria.

41. Niclas *Bawer*, shearer and bell-ringer, Catharina.
42. Niclas *Hock*, cooper, Appollonia.

Shopkeepers	43. Niclas *Forster*, the young, Margreta.
	44. Johannes *Kremer*, Elisabeth.
Blacksmiths	45. Ludwig, Catharina.
	46. Hans *Torr*, Catharina.

47. *Müller* Jacob, carpenter, Barbara.
48. Peter *Moch*, tinsmith, Margreta.
49. *Schüslers* Adam, straw-cutter, Elisabeth.

Shepherds	50. *Scheffer* Henrich, Cathrein.
	51. *Rheman*, Engel.
	52. *Martin*, Barbara.
	53. *Braunhans*, Barbara.
	54. Johannes, Catharina.

f. 48	
Bakers	55. Johannes *Heintz*, Catharina.
	56. Johannes *Durr*, Barbara.
	57. Michel *Heckman*, Anna.

Carters	58. Johan *Pfeil*, Elisabeth.
	59. *Müllers* Johann, Anna.
	60. *Josten* Johann, Catharina.
	61. *Faist* Hans, Catharina.
	62. Cunrad *Hock*, Margreta.
	63. Niclas *Jost*, Barbara.
	64. *Hamel* Johann, Gertraud.
	65. *Schneiders* Hans, Barbara.
	66. Ja(c)ob *Stiel*, Elisabeth.
	67. *Moos* Peter, Catharina.
	68. *Schneiders* Peter, Anna.
	69. *Josten* Jacob, Catharina.

Carters	70. *Becker* Jacob, Anna.
	71. *Rosen* Mathias, Barbara.
	72. *Tobias* Johannes, Elisabeth.
	73. *Bawers* Henrich, Catharina.
	74. Michel *Schlecht*, Barbara.
	75. Hans *Hock*, Margreta.
	76. *Scher* Johann, Maria.
	77. *Schneiders* Mathies, Catharina.
	78. *Freysen* Johann, Anna.
	79. Peter *Hock*, Elisabeth.
	80. Simon, Catharina.
	81. *Moos* Niclas, Barbara.
	82. Tobias *Barborn*, Maria.
	83. *Closen* Hans, Catharina.

f. 48 v.	
	84. *Schneiders* Henrich, Engel.
	85. *Kais* Wolff, Maria.
	86. *Braun* Niclas, Elsa.
	87. Johannes *Biel*, Anna.

"Einspennige" (Owning one yoke)
- 88. Johannes *Strunck*, Maria.
- 89. Jacob *Strunck*, Magdalena.
- 90. *Bier* Johan, Cathrein.
- 91. *New* Clos, Geza.

Widowed people.

1. *Juden* Jacob.
2. *Jeckels* Elsa.
3. *Steines* Agnes.
4. Jacobs *Gall*, Barbara.
5. *Gallen* Barbara.
6. *Kuh* Engel.
7. Margreta.
8. *Schaffer* Hans.
9. *Steines* Agnes.
10. *Bawers* Clos.
11. *Tobias* Maria.
12. *Barborn* Eva.
13. *Jörigen* Anna.
14. Elisabeth *Scherr*.
15. *Scherers* John.

f. 48. v.

Ruessberg.

1. *Schneiders Culman*, court official and censor, Barbara.

Woolweavers
- 2. *Jost*, Margreta.
- 3. Moses *Frisch*, Maria.
- 4. *Caspars* Bernhart, Maria.
- 5. Henrich *Dickes*, Catharina.

6. Johan *Bibel*, wool-weaver and shopkeeper, Martha.
7. Melchoir *Scholl*, tailor, Anna.
8. *Jung Hansen* Jacob, shoemaker, Barbara.
9. *Jung*, Hans, roofer, Barbara.

f. 49.
10. Peter *Dickes*, brick-layer, Margret.
11. Barten *Culman*, brick-layer, Cathrein.

Carters
- 12. Fritten *Culman*, Barbara.
- 13. Caspar *Schelhorn*, Anna.
- 14. *Schwa* . . . Barnhart, Barbara.
- 15. Franz *Cappes*, Appolonia.
- 16. Henrichs *Caspar*, Maria.
- 17. *Schu* Peter, Agnes.
- 18. Strumen *Merten*, Maria.
- 19. *Schneiders* Hans, Maria.

"Einspennig" (Owning one yoke)
- 20. Martin *Heckman*, Catharina.
- 21. *Hamans* Peter, Barbara.
- 22. *Hamans* Hans, Barbara.
- 23. *Steines* Agnes.
- 24. Hans *Strum*, Künigund.
- 25. *Mullers* Johan, Cathrina.

26. *Barben* Adam, straw-cutter, Margreta.
27. Endres *Klein*, Maria.
28. Bast *Knap*, Catharina.

29. Mattheis *Müller*, Catharina.
30. *Hirt* Endres, shepherd, Sinn.

Widowed people.

1. *Trein.*	4. *Bielen* Barbara.
2. *Isten Peter.*	5. *Balthas* Margret.
3. Margreta.	

f. 49 v.

Aulenbach.

1. *Michels* Johan, court official and censor, **Elisabeth.**
2. Henrich *Kirsch*, tailor, Elisabeth.
3. *Matthias*, linen-weaver, Elisabeth.
4. *Theoboldt*, shopkeeper, Elisabeth.
5. *Backes* Bernhart, Catharina.
6. *Frantz*, Appollonia.
7. Jeorg *Flick*, Appollonia.
8. Adam *Heilman*, Appollonia.
9. *Garter* Bernhard, Gertrude.
10. Hans *Dorn*, Catharina.

Carters { (items 5–10)

11. *Claus*, innkeeper, Margreta.
12. *Emerich*, Elisabeth.
13. *Hennes*, Hans, Gertrude.
14. Heinz *Dorn*, widower.

Manbechel.

1. *Helpeschner* Johan, court official and censor, Elisabeth.
2. Hans *Schneider*, tailor, Margret.
3. Peter *Bretter*, joiner, Otilia.
4. *Joichims* Hans, blacksmith, Getza.
5. Michel *Fock*, miller, Maria.
6. Johannes, Elisabeth.
7. *Veltin*, Elisabeth.
8. *Clos*, Elisabeth.

Shepherds { (items 6–8)

9. Elisabeth, widow.
10. *Heylmans* Cathrein.

f. 50

11. *Gerlachs* John, Martha.
12. *Leisen* Hans, Catharina.
13. *Leisen* Niclas, Anna.
14. *Junghausen* Theus, Elsa.
15. *Bulen* Cunrad, Margreta.
16. *Bulen* Niclas, Catharina.
17. *Treinen* Best, Els.
18. *Martins* Johann, Elisabeth.

f. 50

19. *Verein* Cunrad, Catharina.
20. *Bulen* Johann, Elisabeth.
21. Hans *Thom*, Catharina.
22. *Junghansen* Johann, Appollonia.
23. Matthias *Jeckel*, Engel.
24. Niclas *Helpescher*, Engel.
25. *Caspars* Jacob, Cathrina.

26. *Treinen* Gerhardt, Engel.
27. *Heintzen* Niclas, Elisabeth.
28. *Bastians* Theobald, Anna.
29. *Stürmen* Hans, Catharina.
30. *Würtz* Hansen Cunrad, Cathrina.
31. Barbara, widow.
32. *Trauden* Cathrein, widow.
33. Maria, widow.
34. *Heintzen* Johann, widower.
35. Eva, widow.

Grünenbach.

1. *Schmids* Hans, court official, Elisabeth.
2. Eucharius *Faust*, censor, Margreta.
3. Hans *Schmidt*, blacksmith, Maria.
4. *Cuntzen* Peter, Agnes.
5. *Gerharts* Hans, Catharina.
6. *Felsen* Hans, Appollonia.
7. *Gerharts* Peter, Anna.
8. *Gerharts* Jeckel, Elisabeth.

Carters
{ 9. *Bruders* Merten, Elisabeth.
{ 10. Conrad *Kriger*, Maria.

11. *Emerich*, Barbara.
12. *Cuntzen* Niclas, Anna.
13. *Emerichs* Hans, Eva.
14. Niclas, innkeeper, Catharina.

Rohnberg.

1. *Peters* Johann, court official, Catharina.
2. *Schlossers* Hans, censor, Elisabeth.
3. Hans *Pies*, linen-weaver, Anna.
4. *Müller* Peter, miller, Anna.

Carters
{ 5. Hans *Schardt*, Catharina.
{ 6. Philips *Schart*, Margreta.
{ 7. *Wilhelms* Jeckel, Elisabeth.
{ 8. Claus, Margreta.

Shepherds
{ 9. Andries *Pies*, Anna.
{ 10. *Kuh* Claus, Barbara.

f. 51
11. *Boon* Hans, Sinn.
12. *Hansmans* Heydrich, Margreta.
13. Johanns *Birck*, Agnes.
14. *Birck* Barbara.

Fronhausen

1. Peter *Hoffmans*, court official and censor (widower)
2. Johan *Schmidt*, blacksmith, Catharina.
3. Johann *Schuster*, shoemaker, Engel.
4. Johan *Noper*, Elisabeth.
5. *Danst*, Appollonia.
6. *Kirschen* Hans, Clara.

    7. *Kirschen* Johann, Engel.
    8. *Hoffmans* Niclas, Elsa.
    9. Niclas, Appollonia.
  10, *Philips*, Catharina.
  11. *Gödman*, Catharina.
  12. Peter *Haas*, Catharina.
  13. *Kessel* Hans, coppersmith, Elisabeth.
  14. Niclas *Ort*, shepherd, widower.

f. 51 v.   *Denweyler, Fronbach.*

    1. Johannes, censor, Catharina.
    2. *Davids* Jacob, Catharina.
    3. Jonas, Maria.
    4. Claus, Appollonia.
    5. *Fehl* Hans, Agnes.
    6. David, Anna.
    7. *Simons* Johannes, Maria.
    8. *Schultheissen* Johan, Maria.
    9. *Diel*, Catharina.
  10. *Gerharts* Johann, Lena.
  11. Niclas *zu Alben*, Margreta.
  12. Henrich *Kautz*, shepherd, Agnes.
  13. *Schultheissen* Hans, Appollonia.
  14. *Gerharts* Johannes, Engel.
  15. Fridich, shepherd, Sara.
     Widows: Maria, Elisabeth, Elisabeth.

Ertzweyler.

Censor   1. Simon *Doll*, Catharina.
    2. Johan *Bawer*, Barbara.
    3. *Kuhn* Anthes, Otilia.
    4. Abraham *Hinckler*, Catharina.
    5. *Davids* Hans, Appolonia.
    6. *Otilien* Niclas, Barbara.
    7. *Mackhen*, Johann, Ferena.
    8. *Bock*, Sinna.
    9. Jacob *Doll*, Elisabeth.

f. 52.   *Langenbach.*

    1. *Heydrich*, censor, Anna.
    2. *Michel*, Maria.
    3. *Thomas*, Elisabeth.
    4. *Peter*, Anna.
    5. *Philips*, Appolonia.
    6. Johann, miller, Eva.
    7. Claus, miller, Elisabeth.
    8. Wilhelm, shepherd, Agnes.
     Widowed people: Cleinhans and **Maria.**

30   *Genealogical Society Publications*

fol. 62	List of the inhabitants of the two Chapels *Bersch-* and *Eckharsweiler* [1] in the parish Baumholder, noted on May 14th, anno 1609.
Brick-layer	*Welsch*, Hans, Elisabeta, 3 children: Hans Peter, Nicolaus, Maria.
	Debolt *Schneider*, widower, 1 daughter Su(s)anna (!).
	Cornrad (!) *Schneider*, Catharina.
	Conen Jacob, widower.
	New Hans, Barbara, 1 daughter Barbara.
Linen-weaver	Hans *Weber*, Maria, 3 sons: Hans, Peter, Nickel.
	Debolts Peter, Barbara, 2 daughters: Elisabeth, Catharina.
	Debolts Gehames, Anna, 1 daughter: Elisabeth.
	Nickel *Reis*, Barbara, 2 children: Catharina, Hans Peter.
	Kleinhans *Schleich*, Engel, 3 children: Nickel, Heinrich, Catharina.
Assistant judge	*Alberts* Claus, widower.
	Clausen Hans, Clara, 3 sons: Johannes, Peter, Nickel.
Miller	Martin *Culman*, Elisabeth, 1 daughter: Maria.
	Geham (!) *Gelzleichter*, Margreta.
	Friderich, Elisabetha, 1 son: Johannes.
Mayor and censor	Peter *Culman*, Catharina.
	Peter *der Jung Kulman*, Barbara, 4 children: Johannes, Maria, Anna, Catharina.
fol. 63.	
Shepherd	*Hans*, Margreta, 1 child: Maria; 1 servant: Hans.
	Hans *Schneider*, Barbara, 9 children: Matheus, Peter, Gehames, Johannes, Margareta, Madalena, Anna Maria, Catharina, Barbara.
	Paulus *Schneider*, Elisabeta, 1 daughter: Elisabeta.
	Nickel *Golzenlichter*, Barbara, 1 daughter: Maria.
Cowherd	Peters *Nickel*, widower, Susanna, 3 children: Maria, Peter, Hans.

Foren.[2]

	Beiers Hans, Catharina, 8 children: Nickel, Johannes, Elisabeta, Catharina, Maria, Barbara, Apolonia, Hans Peter.
	Hans *Kell*, Apolonia, 3 children: Johannes, Nickel, Elisabeta.
Court Official	Lorenzen Geham, Maria, 5 children: Peter, Catharina, Elisabeta, Nickel, Anna.
	Caspars Nickel, Catharina, 2 children: Maria, Barbara.
	Lorenz Maria, widow. *Scheffer* Debolt's wife, Catharina, 1 son: Hans Peter.

---

[1] Berschweiler and Eckersweiler, northwest, respectively north of Pfeffelbach.

[2] North of Berschweiler.

zu Linden.[1]

Bullen Nickel, Margret.

Neiw, Hans, Agnes, 1 daughter: Elisabeta.

Messen Hans, Ottilia, 5 children: Anna, Barbara, Nobrae(!), Hans, Johannes.

Mettweiler.

Censor — Hans *Hoffman* Catharina.

Nickel *Hoffmann,* Maria, 5 children: Nobrae, Barbara, Hans, Nickel, Peter. Servant: Johannes.

Bron Adam, widower.

Blacksmith — Jacob *Schmidt,* Eva, 2 children: Johannes, Barbara. Servant: Windel.

Sebastianus *Keller,* Nobrae, 4 sons: Nickel, Johannes, Peter, Jacob,—servant: Steffan.

Hans *Reis,* Anna, 2 children: Thomas, Ebert. Servant: Hans.

''Scheffer'' — Johannes Scheffer, Catharina, 4 children: Johannes, Elisabeta, Apolonia, Matheus.

Linen-weaver — Johannes *Jacoby,* Maria, 3 children: Barbara, Nickel, Sebastian.

Eckhersweiler.

Hans *Kolman,* Barbara, 4 children: Gehannes, Barbara, Margreta, Johannes. Servants: Peter, Margreta.

Matheis *Veltin,* Christian, 2 sons: Johannes, Hans Peter.

Court official — *Clasen* Nickel, Catharina, 4 sons: Johannes, Dilman, Hans Peter, Gehannes. Servants: Hans, Maria.

Hans *Seibert,* Ottilia, 3 children: Catharina, Barbara, Gehannes. Servants: Nickel, Maria.

Court Official — *Colman* (no Christian Name), Agnes, Servants: Peter, Hans, Jacob, Barbara.

Frizen Peter, Elisabeta, 3 children: Catharina, Johannes, Bartholomey. Servant: Ottilie.

Assistant judge — Hans *Braun,* widower.

Junghans *Braun,* Elisabeth, daughter: Elisabeth. Servant: Nickel.

Court official — *Peters* Hans, Elisa.

Peter, *Peters* Hansen son, Elisabeta, 2 children: Catharina, Johannes. Servant: Gehames.

''Scheffer'' — Nickel *Scheffer,* Apolonia. Servants: Johannes, Margreta.

Hans *Kiehiert,* Madalena.

---

[1] North of Berschweiler.

The husbands, wives, sons and daughters living in the village Achtelsbach:

Wool-weavers	Michel *Krais*, Katharina,	1 son,	2 daughters.
	Mayrs Adam, Alata,		2 daughters.
	Bastian Mathes, Maria,		3 daughters.
	Mayrs Hanns, Katharina,	4 sons,	2 daughters.
	Peters Hanns, Anna,	2 "	1 daughter.
Bell-ringer	*Fritschen* Wendel, Elss,	3 "	2 daughters.
" Scheffen "	*Roden* Mathes, Getz.		
Cooper	*Roden* Lorentz, Madelena.		
Cooper and censor	*Gödtmann* Bender, Maria.		
Cooper	*Niklas* Sohn, Margreta.		
Wheelwright and "Scheffen"	*Schwenkhen* Clas, Getz,	2 sons,	3 daughters.
Shopkeeper	·Hanns *Hes*, Getz,		2 daughters.
Cooper and beer-brewer	Peter *Hoffman*, Margreta,	2 sons.	
" Mayer "— farmer	*Junghanns*, Anna.		
	Linckers Johannes, Barbell,	1 son.	
	Sielmans Hanns, Katharin,	2 sons.	
Blacksmith and "Scheffen"	*Schwenkhen* Michel, Engel,	2 sons,	1 daughter.
	Schühe Hanns, Maria,	1 son,	2 daughters.
Baker and innkeeper	*Engelbenders* Johann, Agnes,	2 "	3 "
	Becker Clas, Kätharin.		
	Schwenkhen Melcher, Katharin,	1 "	1 daughter.
Cooper	Wendell *Bender*, Philippa.		
" Scheffer "	*Kleinhanns*, Engel,		3 daughters.
Cowherd	*Kühe* Peter, Anna,	1 "	1 "
Bailiff	Niclas *Grub*, widower.		
	Peters Caspar, widower.		
	Theis *Becker*, widower.		
	Mäyrs Ludwig, widower.		
	Basten Anna, Widow.		
	Schneiders Anna, widow.		
	Schmidt Getz, widow.		

and 8 male servants and 3 female servants.

Censor	Adam *Schmidt*, Getz,	1 son,	1 daughter.
Wheelwright	*Melchers* Hanns, Margreta,		4 daughters.
	Langhanns, Elisabeth,		2 daughters.
	Ludwig *Staud*, Barbell,		1 daughter.
	Hirt Hanns, Engel,	1 son,	1 female servant.

---

[1] Meckenbach, northwest of Nohfelden.

Linen-weaver	*Lamberts* Claus, Agnes.	1 son,	1 male servant.
	Heinzen Ludwig, widow, Els,	2 sons.	
	Linckers Els, widow.		
	Schühe Melchers Els.		

Traunen.[1]

"Leyendecker" (Slaterer)	Peter *Köler*, Elisabeth.		
Cowherd	*Frantz* Hanns, Barbel.		
Thatcher	*Frantzen* Peter, Alat.		
Turner	*Cuntz* Thomas, Maria,	1 son.	
	Cuntz Niklas, Katharin,		2 daughters.
Assistant judge	*Cuntz* Claus, Engel,	3 sons,	1 daughter.
Shopkeeper	Michel *Hes*, Agnes.		
Censor	Anthes *Spreyr*, Barbel,	1 son.	
	Paulus *Platz*, Anna.		
	Niklas *Cräs*, Maria.		
Miller	Carius *Schweitzer*, Eva.		1 female servant.
Merchant	Johannes *Cuntz*, Maria.		
Carpenter	Debolt *Lang*, Maria,	3 sons.	
Cooper	*Thüngis* Enders, Eva.		
Cooper	*Klein* Claus, Barbel,	1 son,	2 daughters.
	Göbeln Peter, Maria,		2 daughters.
Locksmith	Jacob *Freytag*, Katharin,	2 sons,	2 daughters.

fol. 66	*Ellweiler.*		
	Rudolf *Schuster*, Anna,	3 sons,	2 daughters.
	Thomas *Zimmerman*, Katharin,	1 son,	1 daughter.
	Simon *Kessler*, Anna,	2 sons.	
Shepherd	*New* Niklas, Demüt,	3 sons,	1 daughter.
Cooper and censor	Johannes *Grüb*, Margret,	2 sons,	1 female servant.
	Claus *Aysell*, Katharin,	1	" "
	Johannes *Aysell*, Barbell.		
	Hanns *Schmeyr*, Anna.		
	Peter *Schmeyr*, Eva,	2 sons,	1 daughter.
	Martin *Bender*, Gertraud,		3 daughters.
	Müllers Niklas, Maria.		
"Scheffen"	Anthes Niclas, Els,	1 son,	1 daughter, 1 male servant.
Carpenter	Caspar *Lorch*, Maria,	2 sons,	2 daughters.
Cooper	Thomas *Bruch*, Appell,	1 son,	3 daughters, 1 male servant.
	Hans *Schwenckh*, Anna,	3 sons,	2 daughters.
	Schneiders Anna, widow,	1 son,	1 daughter.
	Kriegers Els, widow,	1 son,	1 daughter, 1 daughter.
	Müllers Greta, widow.		
	New Anna, widow.		
	There are 15 houses.		

---

[1] Northwest of Meckenbach.

REPORT ABOUT THE HOUSES AND INHABITANTS
FOUND IN THE PARISH.

Wolffersweiler,

when it was visited on May 17th and 18th, anno 1609.

f. 74.

1. Johann *Göbel*, widower, mayor and censor, has in his
   house his son-in-law Hans *Luder*, a linen-weaver and
   his wife Margret. Sons of the son-in-law:
   > Nickel, Jörg is wandering, Johannes major, Jo-
   > hannes minor.

   Daughters: Engel, Maria, Appel.
2. *Lauwer* Jacob, a "Schöpfen" and innkeeper, Els
   his wife. (Her) son: Hans, his wife Agnes, their
   daughter Els. Male Servants: Thison, Martin, "both
   of the papacy" (catholic).
3. *Bietels* Hans, widower, a "schöpfen" and wool-
   weaver, his son-in-law Hans, a baker, the latter's
   wife Maria, their daughter Anna.
   > The old's son: Henrich.

   Male servant: Thison ex papàtu (catholic).
4. Henrich *Menger*, widower, a "schöpfen" and linen-
   weaver, whose son: Hans, his wife, Margreta, their
   son: Johannes. Male servant: Matthes ex papàtu.
   The female servant: Els, Stephan's daughter of this
   village.
5. Jacob *Köl*, censor and tanner, his wife Els. Sons:
   Hans and Jacob. Daughters: Ketter and Maria.
   The child of the son: Hans Nickel.
6. Hans *Müller*, censor and miller, his wife Maria.
   Sons: Hans and Michel, daughter: Els. Michel the
   cousin, old and unmarried.
7. Clos *Becker*, a baker, his wife Els. Son: Michel.
   Daughters: Engel, Agnes, Barbel, Anna, Maria.
8. *Hermans* Jacob, a brick-layer, Maria.
   > The son-in-law: Hans *Müller*, Barbel, have 2
   > sons: Martin, Hans *Jacob*, the daughter: Els.
   > Jacob's daughter: Barbel. Male servant: Jacob
   > of this village.
9. *Michel Nofelser*, widower, a linen-weaver and Hans
   "weilerischer meier." Son: Michel.
   > Male Servant: Wendel ex papàtu, female ser-
   > vant: Ketter von Selbach, in feudal service.
   > The son-in-law: Johannes, a dyer. The wife:
   > Barbel. The children: Hans, Maria, Els.
10. *Barthel Schumacher*, a shoemaker, the wife Barbel,
    daughter Anna. The male servant: Hans, his grand-
    child.

f. 75

11. *Johann Göbel minor*, Barbara: Hans Wilhelm, Els.
    Male servant: Petter of Baumholder.

12. *Bietels Michel,* Barbel: Hans, Nickel, Maria, Anna, Margret.
13. *Bast Rohtfuohs,* tanner and farmer, Ketter: Barbel, Els, Maria, Agnes, Ketter.
14. *Bauwers Frit,* linen-weaver, Els.
15. *Linden Wilhelm,* tanner, Margret: Michel, Els, Ketter, Christina. Male Servant: Michel ex papatu.
16. *Hans Bär,* baker, Barbel: Hans Jörg, Hans Nickel, Appel, Barbel. Female servant: Trein of Selbach, in feudal service.
17. *Jacob Kob,* a blacksmith, architect, Anna: Johannes, Michel, Maria. Male servant: Wolff of Ellweiler.
18. *Schneider Michel,* a wool-weaver, Clara: Hans, Barbel, Margreta.
19. *Becker* Hans, baker and innkeeper, Agnes: Stoffel, Petter, Ketter, Eva.
20. *Stephans Hans,* farmer, Els.
21. *Linden Adam,* farmer & tanner, Ermel: sons: Johannes major, Johannes minor; Christina the female servant ex papatu.
22. *Hans Horrenberger,* bell-ringer, Els. Christman, wandering, Hans Jacob, Nikolaus, Clara. Female Servant: Anna of Sellbach, in feudal service.
23. *Beckers Jöb,* cooper, Ketter: Els, Ketter, Barbel. The mother, widow, Sophie, the brother Petter, the sister Margret.
24. *Petter Gudendahl,* tailor, Sinn(a): 2 sons, 5 daughters: Hans, Petter, Engel, Anna, Margreta, Maria, Christina.

f. 76

25. *Christmans* Johannes, day-labourer, Trina: Hans, Hans Michel, Maria.
26. *Linden* Clos, tanner, Els, 3 sons, 2 daughters: Hans major, a clerk, Hans minor, item Thilman, Ketter, Els.
27. Stephan *Gödman,* wool-weaver, Els, 2 daughters: Ketter, and Els serves in the village.
28. Hans Horch, baker, Els, 2 sons: Jörg, Hans.
29. *Wendels* Appel(onia), widow, daughter: Maria, whose husband Hans Thür is in Baumholder,[1] her daughter: Barbel.
30. *Schumachers* Cetter, widow, 1 son, 2 daughters: Johannes, Els, Maria.
31. *Kremer* Marie, a shopkeeper's widow. Female servant: Margret of Ellweiler.
32. Henrich *Buch,* shepherd, Els, item a female servant.
33. Hans *Buch,* cowherd, Eva, 2 daughters: Els, Engel.

---

[1] They lived separately, and she had run away from her husband (fol. 97).

34. Clos *Keiser,* egenus Agnes.
35. Martinus *Hoffius,* Cuselanus, minister, uxor, Anna, filius Joanes, filiae: Christina, Anna Margreta, mater pastoris: Margreta, widow, ancillae Sophia et Elisabetha.

f. 76 v.   *Nofelden.*

Johannes *Kneupel,* cellarman ("keller"), Susanna, 3 sons: Hans Friederich, studet Hornbaei, Hans Albert, Hans Jacob. Male servant: Jörg the clerk, Bast the miller, Gödman the shepherd. Female Servants: Barbel, Anna, Ketter (name missing), Eva.

House-owners.

1. *Bungerts,* Johannes, Censor, Agnes, 2 sons, 3 daughters: Clos, Jacob, Sin, Christina, Susanna.
2. *Naumans* Adam, brick-layer, Barbel: Els.
3. *Hans Winckenbacher,* shoemaker, Getz, 2 sons, 2 daughters: Jacob, Hans, Clara, Margreta.
4. *Webers* Clos, "schöpfen" and innkeeper, Ketter, 1 son, 2 daughters: Martin, Eva, Ketter. The son-in-law Petter, a baker, the wife Barbel.
5. *Caspers* Hans, linen-weaver, Els, 1 son: Nickel. The mother, widow, Els; a male servant from Soetern.
6. Michel *Liebmann,* blacksmith, Maria, item a young daughter, the son Johannes, blacksmith, Maria uxor, his daughter Eva, item Jörg the young son. Male servant Wendel of Wolf-f(ersweiler).

f. 77. 7. Jacob *Leismann,* baker and innkeeper, Els, 3 sons: Hans, Mans Jörg, Nickel.
8. *Peters* Hans, wheelwright, Maria, 3 sons: Matthes, a cooper, Michel, Martin.
9. *Naumans* Hans, farmer, Barbel, 1 son Michel, item two daughters: Barbara item another one, Getz his sister-in-law.
10. *Lawers* Johann, "schöpfen", Barbel. The son-in-law *Schneiders* Hans a linen-weaver, the wife Els. Sons: Hans Jörg, Clos, Petter; the daughter, Ehl. Female servant: Els of Wallenhausen.
11. *Jacob Foos,* Eva. Brothers: Nickel, linen-weaver, Thomas. The sons: 2. item a maid Barbel, of Wallenhausen.
12. *Jacob Bittel,* the old, widower, his son Michel, the wife Maria, 1 son, 1 female servant of Deckenhart.
13. Hans *Frist,* "schöpfen" & tanner, Ketter, 1 son: Hans Jörg, the wife Barbel. An apprentice Simon of Sahrbrücken.
14. Nickel *Heckman,* Getz, 2 sons, 2 daughters: Johannes Michel, Els and another one.

15. Hans *Bittel* the young, Els, 4 sons: Jacob, Hans Michel, Petter, Hans Jörg.

f. 77 v.
16. Matthes *Schmit*, faber, Els, 3 sons, 2 daughters: Hans, Enoch, Michel, Christina and another one.

17. Dionisius *Cleburg*, carpenter, Magdalena, 1 son.

18. *Wolff*, forester, widower, 4 sons, 2 daughters: Hans, Michel, Carlen, Michel, 2 daughters, female servant Eva of Gundesweiler.

19. Heilmann *Lawer*, a tanner ("rodgerber"), widower, son Nickel, the wife Agnes, item Michel, nothus de demortuo filio: Nickels' daughter Susanna, the grandchild Hans. Jörg, Anna Elisabeth the female servant, catholic.

20. Theis *Kühirt*, Ketter, 6 sons, 4 daughters.

21. Johann *Schaffhirt*, Margret, 2 sons.

Wallenhausen.

1. *Ullhansen* Clos, censor and farmer, Anna, the daughter Ehl, male servant Hans, catholic, the female servant Agnes of Meckenbach.

2. Junghansen *Wendel*, farmer, Margret.

3. *Schneiders* Clos, farmer, Ehl, 3 sons, 1 daughter: Petter, Hans, Clösgen, Ketter.

f. 78
4. *Heüne* Johann, farmer and innkeeper, Agnes, the son-in-law Clos, a linen-weaver, the wife Ketter, sons Clos, Petter, daughters Els, Margred, Eva, Ehl.

5. Petter *Labacher*, brick-layer, Sin, 2 sons, 2 daughters: Niclas, Petter, Ehl, Els.

6. Hans *Heün*, farmer, Margret, the son Petter, the wife Els–.

7. *Lorentzen* Petter, widower, farmer, 2 sons, daughters: Johannes major, Johannes minor, Engel, Ketter, Ehl serves in the valley. The brother-in-law Engelen Velt(en), the wife Els.

8. *Thielmans* Petter, farmer, Christina, 1 son, 3 daughters: Niclas (daughters not named).

10. *Wagners* Niclas, carpenter, Els, 4 sons: Velten, Johannes, Haupert and another one.

11. *Corrects* Hans, shoemaker, Anna, 3 sons, 1 daughter: Hans, Petter, Bast, Maria.

12. *Thielen* Bast, brick-layer, Ermel, 2 daughters: Els, Anna Marie.

13. Clos *Spengler*, copper-smith, Maria.

14. *Kremer* Els, widow, sons: Hans, Niclas.

f. 78 v.
15. Stephan *Birck*, shepherd, Ketter, 3 sons, 2 daughters: Petter, Johannes, Johannes junior, Ketter, Eva.

16. Clos *Naw*, widower, farmer, the son Nickel, the wife Engel, her son Petter.

17. *Schützen* Engel, widow, 5 daughters: Els in No-
    felden, Sinn, serves in Allenbach, Ketter in Bersch-
    weiler, Maria, Barbel.
18. *Jörg*, another cowherd, Sinn.
19. Alexander *Dietz* of Ladenbergk, a flayer, Salome his
    wife, the female servant Salome.

Steinberg and Deckenhart.

1. Hans *Heün*, censor and wheelwright, widower, his
   son-in-law Jacob, the wife Cetter, her daughers:
   Barbel, Maria, Els. The female servant Margred,
   catholic.
2. Velten *Schmit*, Engel, 3 sons, 1 daughter: Hans,
   Bast, Clösgen, Gred.
3. *Keisers* Hans, Maria, 3 sons: Hans, Petter, Nickel.

f. 79   4. *Keisers* Jacob, farmer, Maria, the daughter Eva, male
   servant Hans of Riechwiller.

v   5. *Schneiders* Thiel, farmer and tailor, his sisters Ehl,
   Merg and Els.
6. *Hanwendel*, farmer, Maria, her beloved daughter
   Margret. *Hanclos* the brother, the wife Maria, has
   one daughter. *Han* Jacob the brother.
7. *Linckers* Matthes, Engel, 2 sons, 1 daughter: Petter,
   Bast, Ketter.
8. *Linckers* Henrich, carpenter, Ketter.
9. *Sahr* Clos, wheelwright, Künigunda, the son Hans,
   his wife Anna, her son Hans Petter, the daughter
   Eva, item Closen sons: Nickel, Petter, Tiel.
10. *Cuntzen* Maria, widow, the old, the young Maria,
    widow, her sons Junghans, Jacob, Niclas, Hans Jacob,
    Item 1 male servant ex papatu.

Deckenhart.[1]

12. *Künen Baum* Hans, Eva, 3 sons, 4 daughters: Hans,
    Petter, Hans Petter, Künigund, Maria, Els, Barbel.
13. *Kunen* Johannes, widower, farmer, the mother Maria,
    the daughters Anna Maria, Agnes, Anna.

f. 79 v.   14. *Bauch* Velten, farmer, widower, 1 son, 2 daughters:
    Petter, Els, Ketter; Maria, the ''schwerer'' widow.
15. *Schancks* Tiel, uxor Getz, 4 sons: Petter, Hans, Jo-
    hannes minor, Bast.
16. *Schancks* Petter, uxor Ottel, daughter Barbel.
17. *Schneiders* Els vidua, Clos, Bast her sons.
18. *Basten* Clos, shepherd, widower, 2 sons, Michel and
    N. N., 2 daughters: Ketter, Els.
19. *Jörg* the cowherd, Anna, children: Nickel, Johannes
    and 2 daughters.

---

[1] South of Nofelden.

Riechwiller, Kreennest, Mosberg.[1]

1. *Baum* Michel, ''schöpfen'' and cooper, Ehl, 2 sons, Petter, Stoffel, the son-in-law: Hans *Heun*, the wife Maria.

2. *Weissen* Petter, censor, farmer, son Hans, the wife Anna, her son Petter. The son Petter at Achtelsbach, daughter Anna.
   Bart Hans the old, widower. Male servant Petter ex papatu.

3. *Barten* Jacob, cooper, uxor Ketter, 4 sons, 4 daughters: Nickel, Antes, Haupert, Michel, Anna, Maria, Sinn, Barbel, item Anna, a foster-child.

4. *Bonen* Hans, a farmer, uxor Agnes, mater Anna, widow, male servant Hans ex papatu, female servant Maria of Nofelden.

5. Theobald *Voltz*, tinsmith, Anna, filius Hans Jacob, mater Els, widow.

6. *Arets* Antes at *Kreen-Nest*, textor, Getz. His brother's children: Petter and Barbel, male servant Clos Lorentz.

Moosberg.

7. Hans *Heün*, agricola, Maria, 2 sons, 3 daughters: Nickel, Clos, Ketter, Els, Ketter junior.

8. *Baum*, Michel the young, Els; mater Getz, widow; the male servant Jacob, the female servant Barbel ex papatu.

9. *Weissen* Maria, Getz's sister, a widow, has 4 sons: Jacob, Petter, Johannes, Hans Nickel, nothus daughters Ketter, Maria, Clara.

9. Hans Jacob *Spengler*, the shepherd, Barbel, 4 sons: Johannes, Jacob, Hans, Nickel, daughter Christina.

VI. Hierstein and Gebwiller.[2]

1. *Keisers* Petter, agricola et praetor, Barbel, sons Clos, Johannes. Closen Henrich, a linen-weaver, uxor Margret, filius Jacob, Anna, daughter. Eva, widow, male servant: Hans von Nofelden, foster children: Hans, Jacob.

2. Petter *Schmit*, faber, Anna. Male servant: Theobald, female servant: Maria ex papatu.

f. 80 v. 3. Niclas *Bawr*, agricola, widower, butler of the family of Manderschit, daughters: Barbel, Eva, item his stepson: Nickel, faber, uxor Anna, sons: Hans, Hans minor, daughters Sinn, Barbel, item the bailiff's step-daughter Margret, ancilla Margret ex papatu.

---

[1] Richweiler, **southwest of** Wolfersweiler, Masberg as well.

[2] Hirstein and Gebweiler, south of Wolfersweiler.

4. Greten Appel, widow, daughter Barbel, serves on the "Gauw", the son-in-law Michel, textor, uxor Maria, her son Nickel, daughter Barbel.
5. *Junckern* Clos, agricola, Lehna, daughters: Margret, Anna, Soror Barbel, a brother-in-law Barbel, male servant Hans ex papatu.
6. *Sachs* Hans, agricola, widower, daughter Ketter. His stepson Jacob, agricola, uxor Cetter, children: Clos and Barbel. The son-in-law *Zöden* Johannes, uxor Maria, daughters Barbel, Anna.
7. *Jung* Jochen, agricola, Ketter, daughters: Margret at Leitersweiler,[1] Ketter, Eva, Barbel.
8. *Sachs* Nickel, widower, farmer. His son-in-law, also agricola, uxor Ketter, son Hans, serves in a catholic house.
9. Johann *Kuehirt*, uxor Appel, sons: Hans, Petter, daughter Els.
10. *Petters* Johannes, agricola, uxor Margreta, soror Els, male servant Hans of Steinberg.
11. *Zöden* Margret, vidua, son Clos, item 2 daughters.
12. *Hansen* Ketter, widow, son Johannes, a cooper, uxor Margret, has 2 children. Item another son Nickel, uxor Maria, has also 2 children, item the son Lorenz. Item 1 male servant of Eisen.
13. *Hauppert*, a tub-maker, the wife Ermel, has three children.
14. *Zöden* Michel, linen-weaver, Sinn, filius adoptivus Johannes, uxor Barbel, her son Petter, foster-children Clos and Barbel.
15. *Johann Spurck*, shepherd, Eva, children: Stephan, and 1 daughter.

VLI. *Answiller and Stegen.*[2]

1. *Fritzen Jörg*, censor, sartor et agricola, Els, children: Hans, Clos, Agnes.
   The mother Els, widow; famulus Velten.
2. *Heilmans* Hans, wool-weaver, Barbel, son: Clos.
   The cousin Els, widow, male servant Matthes.
3. *Küntz*, Sinn widow, sons: Petter, Michel, daughter: Maria serva ex papatu.
4. *Hasen* Johannes, juror, Barbel, children: Johannes, Ehl, Eva, Maria, male servant Hans ex eodem pago.
5. *Hasen* Engel, widow, Clos, Hans, Jörg, Petter, Barbel sons and daughter.

---

[1] Leitzweiler, near Gimbweiler.
[2] Asweiler, south of Wolfersweiler.

6. *Nabers* Els, widow, the daughter-in-law widow Margred, her children Hans, Eva, Ketter, 2 male servants Petter and Hansung ex papatu.
7. *Stephans* Clos, textor, Eva, children Michel, Anna, male servant Christianus.

Eitzweiler.[1]

1. Hans *Nabacher*, mayor and censor, molitor et agricola, Els. Son-in-law: Hans Lauwer, Anna, uxor, her son Hans, the daughter Barbel, servi Wendel ex papatu, item Hans von Deckenhart.
2. Imch *Burg*, linen-weaver, Eva, famulus Hans Nickel of Nofelden.
3. *Seimets* Johann, Textor, Els, female servant ex papatu, famulus Pettri, feudal subject.
4. *Bietels* Jöb, tanner, Agnes, children: Michel, Maria, Margret, Anna, famulus Hans, famula Appel ex papatu.
5. Jacob *Menger*, textor, Ehl, the son-in-law Nickel, uxor Maria, her sons: Hans Jacob, Hans, daughter Maria, male servant ex papatu.

f. 82

6. *Michels* Anna, widow, the son-in-law Niclas *Heun*, textor uxor Ketter, son Michel, filia Maria.
Item the son Bart Jacob, agricola, uxor Eva, filius Hans and one daughter.
7. *Beckers* Niclas, viduus, his son-in-law Hans, uxor Barbel, sons Michel, Imch, Hans Nickel, famula (missing).
8. The shepherd *Gerhart*, uxor Sinn, daughter Maria.

VIIII. *Rohrbach.*[2]

1. *Keber* Jacob, censor and juror, Margret, step-son: Hans Jacob, textor, uxor Ann, son Michel, Barbel, male servant (not stated), female servant Ketter.
2. *Busch* Niclas, farmer, uxor Martha, sons: Seimit, Johannes, daughters: Engel, Margret, Margret jun., Appel.
3. *Welsch* Mattes, agricola, uxor Maria, the mother-in-law widow, Maria, the son Johannes, male servant Jacob ex papatu, female servant Maria.
4. Johann *Storr*, sartor, Agnes, filia Maria.
5. *Schreiners* Jacob, widow Maria, daughter Barbel, also a widow, son Wilhelm.

---

[1] Eitzweiler, south of Wolfersweiler.
[2] Northwest of Berschweiler.

X. *Rückweiler.*[1]

1. Hans *Hauppeler*, ''göltzer'' and juror, Rorbacher pfleg, uxor Ketter, filii Johannes and Nickel, daughters: Maria, Els, male servant Hans ex papatu, fem. serv. Ketter.
2. Michel *Rohtfuchs*, juror and linen-weaver, Agnes, children: Johannes, Jacob, Nickel, Els.
   Female servant: Els, male servant Michel.
3. *Höten* Jacob, agricola, Barbel, son Jacob, male serv. Martin.
4. *Thielen* Niclas, farmer, Clara, son Petter.
5. *Lahm* Johann, the shepherd, Ketter, children: Hans Petter, Els.
6. *Rohrbacher* shepherd, Lehenhard, cowherd, Melz. Hans the shepherd, Ketter, son Hans Bartel.

XI. *Leitzweiler.*[2]

1. *Closen* Johann, agricola, Maria, sons:
   a. Bast, faber, Barbel, his son Jacob, daughter Eva.
   b. Petter, textor, Clara, sons: Johannes, Hans; the daughters (of Closen Johann) Anna (and) Ketter, uxor Josten Peter's son of Baumholder.
2. *Closen* Michel, farmer, Barbel, son Abraham, uxor Appel, the daughter Barbel, son Johannes, Thomas, daughter Margret.
3. *Lampert*, widower, farmer, sons Niclas, Abraham, daughter Maria.
4. *Schweis* Jacob, farmer, Maria, son Nickel, a blacksmith, uxor Ketter, son Petter, son-in-law Michel, uxor Clara, daughter Anna, Culmann his grandchild.
5. Hans *Schaffhirt*, Ehl, has 5 children.

XII. *Gimbweiler* [3] *and Frudesweiler.*

f. 83

1. Nickel *Scherer*, censor, Maria, sons: Hans Jacob, Petter.
2. *Schultesen* Jacob, farmer, Agnes, children: Johannes, Els, Clara.
3. *Simons* Johannes, farmer, Pheronica, children: Hans Nickel, Margreta.
4. *Geusen* Clos, linen-weaver, Sophia, children: Hans Nickel, Michel, Agnes, Clara.
5. *Imch(en)* Nickel, farmer, Barbel, daughter Ketter, brothers-in-law Johannes, sutor, and Andreas, bricklayer.

---

[1] North, between Wolfersweiler and Berschweiler.

[2] North, between Wolfersweiler and Berschweiler.

[3] Near Wolfersweiler.

6. Johan *Wart*, Linen-weaver, Appel, sons: Nickel, Johannes.
7. *Mattesen* Johann, juror, Appel. Children: Clos, pistor, Hans, Johannes junior, Maria.
8. *Hoet(en)* Michel and his sister Maria, unmarried.
9. Johannes *Raut*, farmer and thatcher, Clara, children: Hans, Barbel, Els.
10. *Knappen* Nickel, textor et agricola, Barbel, children
    a. Andres, uxor Anna.
    b. Mattes, c. Franz, d. Clara, e. Maria.
11. Johannes *Studt*, a baker, Barbel.
    Hans, the brother, Els, son Hans Nickel.
    The mother, widow, Gertraud.
12. Hans *Scherer*, Clara, daughter Elsa.
13. Andres *Schmit*, Getza, son Johannes.
14. Petter *Schaffhirt*, Ketter with 4 children.

f. 104   Catalogus omnium parochialium parochiae.

Lichtenbergensis

domuum quoque seu focorum, itemque liberorum ut et servorum ac famularum in singulis computatio.

104 v.
f. 105   *Castle of Lichtenberg.*

1. The Younker Wolfgang *Blick of Lichtenberg*, Mrs. Maria Salome Blickin.
   3 male servants, 1 horseman, 2 carter's men, 3 female servts.
2. Albrecht *von Günterod*, high bailiff, Maria Magnalena Günterodin née Blickin von Lichtenberg, 3 sons: Hans Wolfgang, Albrecht, Friderich Casimir.
   2 male servants Hans Michel, Cornelius, 3 female servants.
3. Conrad *Meyer*, agricola, Catharin, 2 children: Christophel, Appolonia.
   Agnes, Bastian Meyer's widow, has unmarried children with her.
4. Johannes *Gutscher*, shepherd, Catharina, children: Johannes, Hans Herman, Appel.
5. Friederich *Fröschel*, Margareta, 3 female servants: Helena, Anna Maria, Salome.
6. Tobias *Glaser*, the younker of Blicken's butler, Marget filiae, Elisabeth, Anna Margreth, famula Anna.
7. Georg *Eckhart*, physician or ''Bruchschneider'', Johanna, filii Friederich, Christoffel, filia Johanna Elisabeth.
8. Johann *Wernigk*, country clerk, Catharina, filii Melchior, Friederich, filiae Magdalena, Catharina, servus Gödelman, famulae Maria, Elisabeth, Catharina.
9. Anna *Baldwenin*, née Helfantin, filia Maria Magdalena, famula Barbara.
10. Andrees *Müller*, blacksmith, Isabella.

Thal under Lichtenberg.

f. 106

1. Wilhelm *Baum*, drover, Margreta, filius Hans Adam. Johannes *Decker*, agricola, Maria, filius Hans Daniel, filia Otilia.
2. Johannes *Sprenck*, drover, Catharina, 1 female servant.
3. Johannes *Arweiler*, magistrate servant, Catharina, Margreta Johannis Arweiler's sister-in-law, Catharein, Maria Salome filiae.
4. Hang *Lang*, "der alt Bott" his wife Anna, midwife.
5. Sir *Johann Helffenstein*, doctor juris, Kunigundis, 2 male servants, 4 female servants. Beneficiaries of his are Hans Scherer and his wife Margret of Gumbsweiler.
6. Johannes *Becker*, juror, Agnes. filius Nicolaus, filiae Engel, Margret. Bastian *Becker*, Catharina.
7. Johannes *Schumacher*, shoemaker, Agnes. filii Bastian, Niclaus, filia Margret.
8. Theobald *Heydenspon*, tailor, Margret, 1 male servant.
9. Johannes *Klein*, linen-weaver, Barbel. filii Hanns Jacob, Hans Nickel.
10. Clos *Decker*, farmer, Barbel, filii, Theobaldt, Franz and Hans Michael, filia Catharin.
11. Franz Biersieder, innkeeper, Margret, male servant Stephan, female servant Anna.
12. Johannes *Bernhardt*, viduus.
13. Hans *Michael*, farmer, Barbel.
14. Hans *Thiel*, farmer, Agnes.
15. Hans *Jost*, agricola, Anna.
16. Jacob *Opp*, agricola, Christina, filius Hans Seifried, filia Eva.

f. 107

17. Jacob *Metziger*, censor, Agnes, filii Hans Michael, Nickel, Johannes, Jacob.
18. *Paulusen* Jacob, Elisabeth, filius Johannes, filia Martha.   day-labourer.
19. *Paulusen* Barbel, vidua, filius Johannes.
20. David *Klein*, textor, Agnes. Johannes *Klein*, textor, Christian, filiae Anna, Elisabetha.
21. Jacob *Flock*, miller, Barbel, filii, Bastian, Johannes and Niclaus, filia Barbel.
22. *Müller* Hans, tanner, filia Margret.
23. Hans Jacob *Flock*, constable, Catharina, filii Hans Jacob, Michael, Johannes, Niclos.
24. Hans *Sprenck*, drover, Barbel, famulae Margret, Barbel.
25. Hans *Kübler*, saddler, Agnes, filii Enoch, David.

26. Johannes *Sältzer*, merchant, Margret, filia Elisabeth, 1 female servant.
27. Johannes *Misawer*, censor, Martha, filii Johannes, Tobias, filia Elisabeth, 1 female servant.
28. Hans *Sältzer's* widow Margret, filia Margret.

Hoff Bistart.

1. Jost *Weidman*, merchant, Elisabeth, filius Johannes, Margret, Agnes.
2. Niclas *Gutscher*, day-labourer, viduus, filia Anna Magdalena.
3. Adam *Schäffer*, day-labourer, Catharina.
4. Hanns Jacob *Ebenhoffen*, watchmaker, Barbel. filii Hans Urban, Hans Martin, Hans Melchoir.
5. Clos *Weber*, day-labourer, Elisabeth, filii Hans Valentin, Franz, filia Margret.
6. Daniel *Sieb*, day-labourer, Barbel, filius Hans Conrad, filia Margret.

I Körborn.

1. Jacob *Schramm*, butcher, filius Hans Jacob. Seimet *Schramm*, farmer, Barbel.
2. Hans *Schramm*, farmer, Apollonia, filiae: Agnes, Gölz, Margret.
3. Margret, *Birtel's* widow, filii Jacob, Hans Theobald, filia Margret.
4. Clos *Hirtt*, shepherd, Barbel, filius Hans Jacob, filia Anna Maria.
5. Clos *Thiel*, farmer, Catharein, filii Jacob, Hans Gerhard, Niclas, filia Marey.
6. Jacob *Grimm*, wool-weaver, Margret, filii Nickel, Hans and Jacob, filia Engel. Clos *Grimm*, widower and censor.
7. Hensel *Schramm*, linen-weaver, Margret, filii David, Johannes, filiae Engel, Margret.

f. 108
8. Johannes *Ruprecht*, farmer, Agnes, filia Barbel, 1 male servant.
9. Theobald *Heisel*, farmer, Margret, filii Johannes, Seimet, Nickel, filia Anna.
10. Peter *Reys*, farmer, Catharein, filii Clos, Nickel, Hans, filia Margret.
11. Nickel, *Seimet*, farmer, Margret, filius Johannes, filia Margret, 1 male servant. *Seimets* Jacob, viduus.
12. Clos *Selbacher*, farmer, Sara.
13. Hanns *Scherer*, wool-weaver, Margret, filii Hans Jost, Bastian, Christina et Barbara filiae.
14. Nickel *Bastian*, farmer, Sara, filii Gerhard, Johannes Jacob.

15. Gerhard *Schöffer's* widow Engel, filii, Niclas, Hans Michael.
16. Johannes *Grim*, butcher, Elisabeth.

Rudweiler.

1. Michael *Müller*, molitor, Margreta, filii Hans, David, filia Margret.
2. Nickel *Schneider*, agricola, Margret.
   Hans *Schneider*, agricola, Catharein.
3. Theobald *Decker*, agricola, Catharein, filius Seimet, filiae Christina, Elisabeth.
4. Hans *Schumacher*, sutor, Barbara, filius Hans Jacob, filiae Margret, Catharein, Anna Christian.
5. Hans *Zimmer*, carpenter, Cathrein, filiae Barbara, Maria.
6. Hanns *Glaser*, Barbara, filius Barthol, filiae Appel, Salome.
7. Hanns *Baal*, agricola, Margret, filii Daniel, Hans Martin, filia Margreta.
   Jacob *Thias*, shopkeeper, Salome.
8. Merten *Gigag*, brick-layer, Catharein, filii Hans Adam, Franz, Hans Peter, Jacob, 1 male servant.
9. Job *Braun*, Maria.
10. Barbara, Jonas *Ruden's* widow, filii Michael, Johannes.
11. *Müller* Jacob's widow, filius Hans, a carpenter.
12. Stoffel *Thias*, carpenter, Margret, filii Niclaus, Hans, filia Engel.
13. Leonhard *Rudt*, farmer, Catharein, filii Clos, Hans Jacob, Filiae Catharein, Margret.
14. Thomas *Raudt*, stone-cutter, Margret, filius Niclas, filiae Salome, Catharein, Agnes, 1 male servant.
15. Nickel *Schmidt*, censor. Margret, filii Hans, Peter, filiae Magdalena, Margret, Anna Barbara.
16. *Ruprecht* the shepherd, Margret, filii Hans Jacob, Theobald, filia Margret.
17. Hans *Scherer*, Censor, Catharein, 1 male servant.
    Johannes *Scherer*, agricola, Margret.

In the parish Lichtenberg there are 77 houses in all, with 376 inhabitants.

List of all inhabitants of the parish-church *Concken*, and the number of married couples, children and servants that were found in every house at this time in the 8 villages.

1. Concken	4. Nider Selchenbach	7. Pfedersheim
2. Albsen	5. Langenbach	8. Crofftelbach
3. Herchweiler	6. Heerschweiler	

          Johannes Helffenstein, ecclesiastes Conckanus.
    May 18th, anno 1609.

f. 123   *The village Concken.*

1. Hanns *Weisgerber*, Appollonia, 1 son Wolfgang, 12 years.
2. Abraham *Weisgerber*, Barbara, no children.
3. Johannes *Thurn*, Elisabeth, 2 children: Agnes, 8 years, Abraham, 2 years.
4. Remig *Weisgerber*, viduus, 2 male servants, 1 female servant.
5. Cornelius *Khühirt*, Elisabeth, 2 children: Nickel, 6 years, Margret, 4 years; 2 male servants: Hansen of Schellweiler and Nickel of Albsen.
6. Lenhard *Hirdt*, Engel.
7. Andres *Schüler*, Gertrud, 1 son Hanns, 20 years.

f. 123 v.
8. Bürtel *Faus*, Barbara, 4 children: Barbara, 11 years, Catharina 6, Abraham 5, Engel 2 years; 2 male servants, Debolt & Konrad of Pfeff; 1 female servant, Görgen's daughter of Herschweiler.
9. Johann *Morgenstern*, the innkeeper, old Cathetter, have no unmarried children in their house, only 3 servants, 2 male servants Abraham of Luittelweiler, Johannes of Reichweiler, 1 female servant Margret of Traweiler Hofpach.
10. Bürtel *Frutzweiler*, Margret, 2 children: Theobald, 22, Wendel 18 years.
11. Johannes *Doll*, Catharina, are in the house of their father-in-law, have 3 children: Barbara 4, Catharina 3, Klein Catharin 2 years.
12. Adam *Morgenstern*, Elisabeth, 5 children: Barbara 13, Agnes 10, Catharina 8, Nickel 6, Elisabeth 4 years. 1 male servant Nickel of Wannwegen, 1 female servant Barbel of Concken.

f. 124
13. Johannes *Morgenstern*, Catharina, 5 children: Bürtel 8, Margret 6, Simon 4, Johannes 2, Barbel 1 year.
14. Theobald *Jung*, Catharina, 3 children: Birtel 24, Catharina 9, Margret 5 years.
15. Schüler Johann *Morgenstern*, Agnes, 4 children: Elisabeth 12, Johannes 10, Margret 5, Barbara 3 years.
16. Jost *Hamman*, Catharina, no children, 2 male servants Hanns of Schwolbach, Jost of Welchweiler, 1 female servant Elisabeth of Osterbrücken.
17. Wilhelm *Bauer*, Margret, 4 children: Andressen 22, Nickel 14, Eva 12, Margret 6 years. 1 male servant Niclaus of the Lützenberger district, 1 female servant.
18. Johann *Keller*, Barbara, 2 servants: Hanns of Schellweiler, Clara of Wannwegen.

f. 124 v.
19. Nickel *Keller*, Margreta, this young married couple have no children yet.

20. Hanns *Morgenstern*, Johann the innkeeper's son, Elisabeth, 3 children: Barbelgen 12, Hanns Thebolt 10, Elsgen 4 years, 1 male servant Johannes of Haupertsweiler.
21. Johann *Pfeil*, Künigund, 3 children: Anna Margret 8, Maria Agnes 5, Elisabeth 3 years.
22. Hanns *Keller*, Apollonia, 5 children: Martin 24, Johannes 20, Hanns 28, Catharina 18, Hannsgen 14 years.
23. Kleinhanns *Keller*, Elisabeth, have no children yet.
24. Peter *Schaffhirt*, Varina, 4 children (names not mentioned).

f. 125

25. Johannes *Helffenstein*, clergyman of this village, Anna, have still 7 sons alive: 1. Hans Wilhelm, 2. Johan Chrisostinus, Johan Andreas, Joh. Friedericus, Joh. Anastasius, Albertus and Benjamin. Female servant: Engel of Pfeffelbach.

The village Albsen.[1]

f. 125 v.

1. Nickel *Jung*, Catharina, 1 daughter Catharina 24 years, 1 male servant Hanns of Herschweiler.
2. Nickel *Jung*, filius superioris, Catharina, 1 child Hanns Nickel, 3 years old.
3. Agnes, Clos *Malzbacher's* widow.
4. Johann *Becker*, Margret, 7 children: Eva 18, Claus 15, Nickel 13, Barbel 9, Catharina 7, Hanns 5, Catharina 3 years.
5. Nickel *Becker*, Agnes, 2 children: Hanns 6, Catharina 3 years.
6. Bürtel *Schneider*, Elisabeth, 5 children: Margret 9, Nickel 6, Marta and Anna, twins, 2, Engel 1 year.

f. 126

7. Nickel *Decker*, Marta, 4 children: Appellonia 12, Claus 10, Margret 6, Nickel 4 years.
8. Peter *Heysell*, Catharina, 5 children: Nickel 14, Hanns 12, Bast 9, Simon 7, Agnes 3 years.
9. Johannes *Scheffer*, Catharina, 5 children: Johannes 14, Elisabeth 13, Barbel 3, Catharina ½ years.
10. Claus *Schumacher*, Barbel, 1 child: Nickel 9 years.
11. Simon *Scheffer*, Barbara, 2 children: Elsa 15, Catharina 10 years, 1 male servant: Hanns of Leuttersweiler.
12. Nickel *Scheffer*, viduus, is in his children's house.
13. Simon *Decker*, Barbel, no children, female servant: Apellonia, Nickel Decker's daughter of Albsen.
14. Hanns *Matzenbacher*, Barbel, no children, 1 male servant Nickel is his wife's nephew, 1 female servant Anna is his sister.

---

[1] Albessen, south of Pfeffelbach.

15. Michel *Becker*, Engel, 4 children: Appellonia 15, Hanns 9, Margret 5, Hanns Wilhelm 2 years.
16. Hyeronimus *Schäffer*, Elisabeth, 1 child: Barbel, 7 years.
17. Hanns *Gruman*, Margret, 1 child: Nickel 2 years.
18. Clos *Becker*, viduus, his male servant Hanns of Herschweiler.
19. Nickel *Schumacher*, Maria, 1 child: Agnes, ½ year.

The village Herchweiler.[1]

1. *Gerlochs* Nickel, (wife not mentioned) 4 children: Agnes 8, Theobald 5, Wilhelm 3, Jacob 1½ years.
2. Simon *Klein*, censor, Margret, 5 children: Catharina, Hanns, Agnes, Margret, Catharina (age not mentioned).
3. *Gerlochs* Hanns, Margret, 4 children: Catharina 20, Simon 18, Barbel 15, Elisabeth 7 years.
4. Johannes *Pfeiffer*, Agnes, 7 children: Agata 24, Hanns 22, Martin 18, Junghanns 16, Maria 12, Reinhard 10, Agnes 7 years.
5. Johannes *Haas*, Engel, 6 children: Otilia 21, Anna 16, Margret 14, Catharina 10, Maria 8, Barbara 5 years.

f. 127 v.
6. Nickel *Müller*, Engel, 2 children (not mentioned).
7. *Schmidts* Hanns, Catharina, 2 children: Theobald 23, Junghanns 14 years.
8. Hanns *Lietzell*, Catharina, 2 children: Anna 6, Simon 4 years.
9. *Neu* Mertens, Hanns defuncti, there are 3 orphans: Margret 14, Junghans 11, Nickel 9 years.

f. 128
Village Nieder Selchenbach.[2]

1. *Mattessen* Adam, Engel, 5 children: Margret 18, Maria 15, Margret 13, Wilhelm 9, Barbara 3 years.
2. Clos *Keller*, Margret, 4 children: Hanns 24, Debolt 18, Agnes 17, Margret 15 years.
3. Jung Hanns *Müller*, Margret, 8 children: Nickel, Theobald, Peter, Engel, Otilia, Agnes, Margret, Catharina (age not stated).
4. Jacob *Gossenberger*, Engel, 3 children (names not stated).

f. 128 v.
The village Langenbach.[3]

1. Johannes *Scheffer*, Apellonia, 3 children: Hanns 10, Agnes 7, Johannes 5 years.

---

[1] West of Albessen.

[2] South of Herchweiler and Albessen.

[3] East of Unter Selchenbach.

2. Caspar *Loch*, Catharina, no children or servants.

3. Birtel *Maus*, Eva, 5 children: Agnes 8, Catharina 7, Elisabeth 6, Hanns Jacob 4, Nickel 1 year.

4. Hans *Müller* viduus, 3 children, 1 male servant Peter of Herschweiler, female servant Apellonia of Albsen. Catharina 5, Maria 4, Elisabeth 2 years.

5. Nickel Schmidt, Engel, 3 children: Agnes 7, Johannes 4, Adam 2.

6. Peter *Scheffer*, Elisabeth, 3 children: Samuel 8, Barbara 6, Johannes 1 year.

7. *Althannsen* Birtel, Gertrud, 3 children: Margreta 5, Johannes 4, Nickel 3 years.

f. 129   8. Wilhelm *Zimmerman*, Sara, 4 children: Johannes 24, Birtel 16, Apellonia 18, Nickel 15 years.

9. *Barbeln* Hanns,[1] Margret, 3 children: Johannes 30 years (2 and 3 not stated).

10. Johannes *Morgenstern*, Christina, no children, Christina has one of her brothers in her house, 16 years old.

11. Hanns *Morgenstern*, Margaretha, 1 child, Margret ½ year.

12. Johannes, Barbeln *Seimets* son, Agnes, 5 children: Johannes 12, Birtel 10, Merten 8, Hensel 4, Gertrud 1½ years.

13. Merten *Meurer*, Agnes, 2 children: Johannes 10, Junghans 6 years.

f. 129 v.   14. Nickel *Thurn*, Agnes, 7 children: Abraham 18, Nickel 16, Johannes 11, Margret 9, Gertrud 6, Agnes 7, Elisabeth 3 years.

15. Theobald *Ludwig*, Agnes, 4 children: Bürtel 7, Johannes 2, Agnes and Margret, twins, ½ year.

16. Peter *Meurer*, Elisabeth, 7 children: Agnes 10, Margret 9, Engel 6, Hans Conrad 4, Christina 3, Marten 2 years, Johannes 5 weeks.

17. Bastian *Schmidt*, Gertrud, 4 children: Adam 9, Christina 7, Agnes 5, Nickel 3 years.

18. Adam *Weber*, Engel, 3 children: Margret 6, Gertraud 5, Johannes 4 years, male servant Hanns, fem. servant Margret.

19. *Apeln* Hans, viduus.

20. *Apeln* Nickel, Margret, no children.

21. Hanns *Büttel*, Agnes, 7 children: Johannes 12, Agnes 10, Elisabeth 8, Nickel 6, Christina 4, Margret 2 years, Adamus Heilmannus 8 days old.

22. Johannes *Morgenstern*, 22 years old, is still unmarried.

---

[1] Compare with No. 12.

f. 130 v.

The village Heerschweiler.[1]

1. *Hensell*, his wife Catharina, have 5 children: Conrad 18, Sara 14, Nickel 7, Agnes 6, Johannes 4 years.

2. *Loch* Gerats vidua, 2 children: Maria 19, Barbel 16 years.

3. Johannes *Loch*, Maria, 1 child Maria 8 years.

4. Johannes *Meurer*, Elisabeth, 2 children: Elsa 6, Otilia 4.

5. Simon *Hielffers*, Catharina, 1 child: Johannes 16 years.

6. Johannes *Hoffacker*, Sara, 6 children: Hans 12, Catharina 8, Nickel 5, Wendel 4, Conrad 2, Catharina 1 year.

7. *Kleinhanns*, viduus, 3 orphans: Otilia 18, Hanns 16, Agnes 14 years.

f. 131

8. Johannes *Klein*, Catharina, 2 children: Catharina 2, Wendel 1 year.

9. Hanns *Weber*, Agnes, 4 children: Apellonia 20, Margret 13, Catharina 12, Margret 8 years.

10. *Metzel* Nickel, Catharina, 4 children: Catharina 7, Nickel 6, Anna 3, Maria 1.

11. Georg *Liesch* (the wife's name is missing), 3 children: Margret 8, Nickel 6, Margret 4 years.

12. Wendel Gerber, Margret, 2 children: Nickel 14, Catharein 8.

13. *Schultheissen* Hanns (the wife's name is missing), 1 male servant Hanns, female servant Appell.

f. 131 v.

The village Pfedersheim.[1]

1. Nickel *Lang*, Appellonia, 1 child: Elisabeth 1 year.

2. Conrad *Lang*, Otilia, 2 servants: Nickel, Catharina.

3. Nickel *Müller*, mayor, Elisabeth, 3 children: Maria 9, Johannes 6, unnamed 3 years, also 3 servants.

4. Engel 2 years, daughter of *Klein* Margret, vidua.

5. *Knappen* Johannes, 4 children: Agnes 14, Johannes 12, Sara 8, Nickel 5 years.

6. Clara, vidua Conrad *Zimmermans*.

7. Agnes, *Metzel* Debolt's widow, 5 children: Hanns 13, Johannes 11, Nickel 7, Jacob 6, Künigund 2 years.

f. 132

8. Debolt *Müller*, Margret, 3 children: Deobalt 8, Wendel 5, Clara 1 year.

9. *Mattes* Hanns, Elisabeth, 4 children: Catharina 10, Conrad 7, Ela 5, Margret 4 years.

10. Remig *Khühirt* (wife not named), 2 children: Conrad 3, Niklas 1 year.

11. Peter (no further names stated), 5 children: Bürtel 14, Nickel 8, Eva 7, Hanns 6, Gertrud 5 years.

---

[1] Herschweiler and Pettersheim, two villages situated close together, south of Konken.

The village Crofftelbach.

1. Nickel *Schmidt*, Elisabeth, 2 children: Appellonia 2, Nickelgen 1 year.
2. Appellonia *Gerats* vidua, 3 children: 1. Debolt 18, Hensgen 10, Johannes 4 years.
3. johannes *Meyrer*, Margret, 1 child 4 years (unnamed).
4. Margret the *Wagner's* (the wheelwright's) widow, 4 children: Hanns 30, Eva 20, Conrad 16, Agnes 12 years.
5. *Schmidts* Hanns, Anna, 8 children: Elsa 17, Appellonia 16, Remmen 15, Nickel 14, Catharina 13, Hans Jacob 12, Hans Nickel 10, Anna 8 years.

f. 133

6. Theobald *Glundt*, Maria, 2 children: Nickel 2, Deboltgen 1 year.
7. Hanns *Becker*, Margreth, 1 child Cattergen 10 years.
8. Johannes *Meyer*, Eva, 4 children: Nickel 8, Johans 6, Hans Heinrich 4, Cattergen 2 years, servants: Jacob of Pfeffelbach, Els.
9. Friderich *Hansmann*, his female servant Maria.
10. *Seymets* Debolt, Eva, 4 children: Hansgen 10, Friderich 8, Johannes 6, Els 2 years.
11. Engel vidua, the above mentioned *Seymets* Debolt's mother.
12. Remig *Müller*, Christina, 4 children: Hanns 30, Johannes 20, Jacob 18, Els 16 years.
13. Nickel *Broch*, Maria, 4 children: Maria 20, Agnes 12, Johannes 10, Hensgen 6 years.

f. 152

Catalogus parochalium Pfeffelbacensium.

Pfeffelbach.

	1. Hans Jungk, censor and court official, Maria,	2 sons.		
	2. Simon *Jungk* and Maria,	1 son,	2 daughters.	
	3. Simon der *Jungkh*, Appolonia,	1 "	2 "	
	4. Nickel *Rämmen*, Agnes,	1 "	2 "	
Carpenters	5. Ruprecht *Halbgewachs*, Christina,	3 sons, 1 daughter.		
	6. Mattias *Lawer*, Eva,	1 son.		
	7. Clos *Zimmerman*, Maria,	3 sons, 1 daughter.		
	8. Lenhard *Zimmerman*, Catharina,	3 "	3 daughters.	
	9. Jacob *Buhl*, Margreta,	2 "	2 "	
	10. Simon *Franckh*, Barbara,	3 "	2 "	
	11. Hans *Heilman*, Barbara,	2 "	5 "	
	Margreta (Heilman) vidua.			
Sartor	12. Hans *Schwarm*, viduus.			
	13. Thomas *Meurer*, Maria,	1 female servant.		
	14. Zacharias *Straus*, Margreta,	3 daughters.		
	Bartholomeus viduus.			

15. Jacob *Thomas*, Margreta, 1 son.
Wilhelm *Straus*, Utilia, 3 daughters.
16. Reinhard *Meurer*, Anna, 3 sons, 2 "
17. Barbara *Rauin*, vidua, 4 "

Censor 18. Hans *Gros*, Engel, 1 male serv., 1 fem. servant.
19. Catharina vidua, 1 fem. servant, 2 sons, 2 daughters.
20. Niclas *Weber*, Catharina, 2 "
21. Clos *Hainsell*, Kinigin, 4 " 4 "
22. Hans *Hainsell*, Margreta, 3 " 4 "
23. Jost *Bittel*, Geetz, 1 son.
Clos *Bittel*, Catharina, 1 daughter.
24. Nickel *Liesch*, censor and court

f. 152 v. official, Utilia, 1 male servant, 1 female servant.
25. Clos *Hengen*, Catharina, 2 sons, 2 daughters.
26. Hans *Besserdich*, Catharina, 3 " 2 "
27. Ludwig *Cardio*, Margreta, 3 " 1 daughter.
28. Job *Weber*, Margreta, 2 " 4 daughters.
29. Hans Schwarm, court official, Catharina,
3 male servants, 1 female servant, 2 sons, 3 daughters.
30. Zacharias *Müller*, viduus,
1 female serv., 2 " 1 daughter.
31. Bastian *Hobacker*, Agnes,
32. Hans *Keller*, Margret, 1 son.
33. Matthias *Schwarm*, censor, viduus.
Paulus *Schwarm*, Margreta, 1 son, 1 daughter.
34. Nickel *Schwarm*, Catarin, 2 sons, 2 daughters.
35. Nickel *Schwarm*, Barbara, 1 son.
36. Seifried *Kerpff*, Catharina, 1 m. s., 1 fem. s., 1 son.
37. Margreta, vidua, 1 male serv., 1 fem. serv.
38. Johann *Straus*, Margreta, 1 female servant.
39. Adam *Eypgen*, viduus, forester, 4 sons, 1 daughter.
40. Nickel *Neuw*, homo senex annorum
105 and Magdaloena.

Reichweiler [1] *Chapel.*

1. Catharina, vidua, has the four following sons living
in this village.

Court official 2. Peters *Hensell*, and Geetz, 4 sons, 3 daughters.
3. Hans *Göltzenleuchter*, censor,
Margreta, 4 "
4. Hans *Michell*, Utilia, 1 son, 1 female servant.
5. Abraham *Petters*, Margreta, 1 son, 4 daughters.
6. Peter *Thielman*, Catharina, have
3 sons who are servants, [also]
1 male servant, 1 female servant.
7. Thomas der *Jung*, Maria, 3 sons, 2 "

---

[1] West of Pfeffelbach.

8. Clos *Schreiner*, Catharina,
   Margreta, vidua,   1 male serv., 1 fem. servant.
9. David *Sorg*, Christina,   1 male servant.
10. Hans *Reitzs*, Catharina,   2 sons, 2 daughters.
11. Thomas der *alt*, Catharina.
12. Hans *Paulus*, Catharina,   2   "
13. Gerloch *Klein*, Catharina,   1 son, 3   "
14. Clasen *Barbel*, vidua.
15. Johann *Klein*, Christina,   3   "

Schwarzerden.

1. Christoffel *Eyffler*, censor, and
   Königin,   2 sons, 4 daughters,
                       2 male servants, 2 female servants.
2. Clos *Knauell*, Ursula,   2 sons, 1 daughter.
3. Hans *Klein*, viduus, has his
   son's wife with her 6 children
   in his house: 2   "   4 daughters.
4. Martin *Becker*, Anna,   2   "   1 daughter.
5. Michel *Müller*, Singen,   3   "   3 daughters.
6. Nickel *Becker*, Barbara,   1 son, 3   "
7. Johan *Weirich*, Appolonia,   4 sons, 1 daughter.
   her son-in-law: Matthias *Schlösinger*,
   sartor.
8. Georg *Weirich*, Geetz,   3 sons.

f. 159   List of all inhabitants of the parish *Cussel*, noted in the
          week before Whitsuntide, anno 1609.

The town of Cussel.

1. Hans *Kümel*, mayor, Anna, female servants: Barl, Jung
   Hansen's daughter of Schelweiler, Agnes, Debolt Culman's daughter of Cussel.
2. Johan *Seibel*, censor, member of a board & juror,
   Katharina, 3 daughters: Otilia, Margreta, Gertraut.
3. Hans *Schan* der elter (the older) member of a board
   and juror, Christina, 2 daughters: Margreta, Engel, 2
   male servants Simon Jung, Nickel Fuchs.
4. Junghans *Becker*, member of a board and juror, Maria,
   female servant Margreta, Noll Müller's daughter of
   Diedelkopf.
5. Nickel *Raut*, censor, member of a board and juror,
   Anna, 1 son Hans, 7 daughters: Els, Barbel, Anna
   Greta, Anna Keterichen, Sara, Martha, Anna Maria.
6. Johannes *Kümel*, member of a board and master of the
   salt-office, Margreta, 1 son Simon Elias, 1 daughter
   Anna, female servant: Sinichen, the tailor's daughter
   of Bersweiler.
7. Hans *Eidt*, member of a board, Margreta, 1 son Hans
   Jacob, 3 daughters: Margreta, Mareylin, Sibilla, Hans
   Jacob Goseberger, boarder, Kettichen Gosebergerin,
   female servant.

8. Simon *Glaser*, paymaster, Anna, 3 sons: Christoffel, Hans Albrecht, Jeremias Abraham, 2 daughters: Johanna Elisabetha, Maria Jacobina, male servant: Peter N. of Walderfangen (catholic), female servants: Margreta, Simon *Heilman's* daughter of Diedelkopf, Otilia, Abraham *Heilman's* daughter of Eheweiler.

f. 159 v.

9. Barbel *Schuch*, rifleman, Katharina, daughter: Margreta.

10. Stoffel *Bartholome*, cooper, Els, 1 son Hans Daniel.

11. Jörg *Walter*, cloth-shearer, Katharina, 2 sons, Hans Jacob, Johannes, 2 daughters Anna, Barbara.

12. Jörg *Trewer*, carpenter, Barbara, 1 son Hans Jörg, 3 daughters Barbelin, Ketichen, Gertraudichen. Henrich Trewer, apprentice.

13. Hans *Jünger*, day-labourer, Barbel, 3 sons Hans Jacob, Hans Nicklichen, Hans Daniel, 1 daughter Barbelichen.

14. Nickel *Schan*, wool-weaver, Katharina, daughter Maria, male servants: Peter *Anthoni*, Henrich *Anthoni*, Hans *Funse*, female servants: Katharina, Peter Jungen's daughter, Johanna spinning-servant.

15. Hans *Achtelsbacher*, day-labourer, Margreta, 2 daughters: Maria, Annalein.

16. Niclas *Windringer*, glazier, Philippina, 2 sons: Hans Jacob, Hans Nickel, 4 daughters: Engel, Barbelin, Anna Greta, Maria Salome.

17. Niclas *Hans*, baker, Barbara, 3 daughters: Margretlein, Anna Salome, Katharina, female servant: Sara of Pfeffelbach.

18. Johannes *Rent*, wool-weaver, Maria, 3 sons: Hans Peter, Hans Jacob, Jonas, 3 daughters: Barbel, Kathareinlin and Margretlein.

19. Johannes *Hof*, glazier, Engel, 1 son Nickel, 3 daughters: Margreta, Sibilla, Otilia.

20. Weigand *Hederich*, tailor, Katharina, 1 son Hans Tobias, 1 daughter Kunigund, apprentice: Debolt Wilbert's son of Ulmat.

21. Martin *Schuch*, tanner, Geza, 1 daughter Anna Margretichen, male servant: Bartel Rentzweiler of Plödesbach, female (maid-) servant: Engelichen, female servant: Els of Hiffelers.

22. Johannes *Schläfeisen*, armourer, Margreta, daughter: Mareylin, apprentice Hans Zehend.

f. 160

23. Jacob *Kaiser*, butcher, Künigund, 4 sons: 2 daughters Hans Jacob, Hans Jost, Hans Nickel, Martinus and Katharina, Brigitta.

24. Peter *Clas*, tanner, Maria, 2 sons Hans Nickel, Hans Michel, female servant: Katharina, Matthes *Teisenbach* of Plödesbach's daughter.

25. Hans *Rentzweiler*, tanner, Barbel, 1 daughter Barbelichen, male servant: Hans *Rentzweiler*, the owner's brother.

26. Johannes *Becker*, beer-brewer, Otilie, son Hans Nickelin, nurse-maid: Elsichen, Hans Streckseisen's daughter.
27. Junghans *Raw*, shoemaker, Margreta.
28. Hans *Seitz*, tanner, 1 son, Henslin, 1 daughter Keterichen, male servant Johannes of Ulmat, female servant Els Seitzin.
29. Hans Peter *Grum*, tanner, Maria Salome, son Hans Wolf, daughter Barbichen, 2 female servants Anna von der Blies, Katharin Bubin.
30. Hans *Stapp*, joiner, Elisabeth, joiner's servant Hans Schmid.
31. Hans *Veltin*, farmer, 2 sons: Hans Enoch, Abraham, 2 daughters Barbelin, Mareylin.
32. Hans *Doll*, day-labourer, Apollonia, 3 daughters: Salome, Anna Gretichen, Christina.
33. Jacob *Kün*, day-labourer, Els, her grandchild: Annichen.
34. Johannes *Wilberger*, slater, Anna, 1 daughter: Mareylin.
36. Daniel *Bair*, shopkeeper, Maria Salome.
35. Hans *Raw*, shoemaker, Katharina, 1 son Hans Jacobichen.
37. Tobias *Bair*, wool-weaver, Anna, 3 sons, Hans Nickel, Hans Jost, Abraham, 2 daughters: Anna Greta, Ursula, apprentice Johannes of Weilerbach, female servant Katharin, Junghansens Metzler's daughter of Pfeffelbach.

f. 160 v

38. Johannes *Wentz*, cowherd, Barbel, 1 son Hans Jacob, 2 daughters Kunigund, Anna Maria, male servant: Abraham, Hans Nawen's son of Eheweiler.
39. Herman *Hirt*, swineherd, Eva.
40. Daniel *Hellrigel*, innkeeper, Katharina, 2 sons Gall, Hans Daniel, 4 daughters Anna, Anna Elisabeth, Künigund, Barbichen, female servant: Margreta, daughter of the Schweitzerin of Cusel.
41. Hans *Sailer*, der junger (the young), linen-weaver, Maria, 1 daughter: Anna Margretichen.
42. Hans *Lawer*, farmer, Margreta, son Hans Philips.
43. Wilerich *Leucht*, butcher, Künigund, 2 sons Hans Jacobichen, Hans Adam, 2 daughters Margreta, Maria Salome, apprentice Hans Jacob.
44. Johannes *Heerman* am Rech, wool-weaver, Maria, 1 son Tobias, 1 daughter Agnes.
45. Hans *Schan* der junger (the young), wool-weaver, Eufrosyne, 1 daughter Anna Margretichen, master-workman: Hans Schan of Quirnbach, apprentice Caspar *Fischer*, female servant Maria, the deceased Bartel's daughter of Körborn.
46. Peter *Heerman* vulgo Schäffer Petichen, farmer, Barbara.
47. Paulus *Haintz*, potter, Anna.
48. Johannes *Rosteuscher*, Engel.

49. *Valentin* Hans, bell-ringer, Brigitta, 4 daughters: Gertraut, Katharin, Kunigund, Barbara.
50. Johannes *Walter*, catch-poll, Barbara, 1 daughter Engel.
51. Hans *Friderich*, cooper, Christina, 1 son Hans Philips.
52. Peter *Friderich*, farmer, Engel, 1 son Hans Veltin, 1 daughter Els.
53. Wendel *Staud*, day-labourer, Maria, 1 son Hans Veltin, 1 daughter Margretlin.
54. Hans Heinrich *Gosenberger*, shearer, Els, 1 son: Johannes, 1 daughter Katereinichen.
55. Johannes *Schweitzer*, brick-layer, Margreta, 1 son: Johanneslin.
56. Johannes *Seitz*, portner (gatekeeper), Barbel, 1 son: Johanneslin.

f. 161

57. Hans Peter *Meurer*, stone-cutter, Engel, 1 son Hans, 3 daughters: Anna Maria, Margreta, Barbichen, male servant Debolt of Krottelbach.
58. Hans *Schwab*, wool-weaver, Katharina, 3 sons Johannes, Hans, Nickel, Hans Lienhart, daughter Barbichen.
59. *Schlos* Hans, lock-smith, Barbel, 1 son Abraham.
60. Lienhart *Michel*, tawer, Agnes, 3 sons: Hans Nickel, Hans Michel, Hans Philips, 2 daughters: Margreta, Kathareinichen.
61. Lorenz *Wagner*, hat-maker, Barbara, 2 sons Hans Martin, Jacob, 2 daughters: Katereinichen, Englichen.
62. Hans *Stoer*,[1] linen-weaver, Engel, 3 sons: Lienhart, Johannes, Hans Jacob.
63. Hans *Heerman*, tailor, Katharina, 2 sons Hans, Nickel, 3 daughters Katharina, Barbel, Margreta, apprentice Hans Jacob.
64. Johannes *Trach*, Linen-weaver, Sara, 3 sons: Hans Nickel, Hans Debolt, Hans Daniel, 1 daughter Barbara.
65. Matthes *Marx*, day-labourer, Katharina, daughter Anna.
66. Simon *Thörr*, brick-layer, Katharein, 1 daughter Margretichen.
67. Jost *Meurer*, stone-cutter, Margreta, 2 sons Hans Bartel, Hans Simon, 1 daughter Ketichen, male servant Nickel of Tirming under the Count of Otweiler.
68. Debolt *Culman*, wool-weaver, Barbara, 4 sons: Nickel, Johannes, Petichen, Hans Jacob.
69. Hans *Sailer*, rope-maker, Els.
70. Martin *Wilerich*, farmer, Katharin, 3 daughters: Katharina, Margretlin, Mareylin.
71. *Teis* Wilhelm, wool-weaver, Katharina, apprentice: Johannes Wendel.

f 161 v.

72. Michel *Zimmerman*, carpenter, Katharina, 1 daughter, Agneslin, master-workman Hans.

---

[1] May be read "Storr".

73. Wiltz *Thörr*, whitewasher, Katharina, 2 sons: Petichen and Martinus, Anna Maria.

74. Nickel *Gerlach*, shoemaker, Margreta, 3 sons: Johannes, Jacob, Martinus, 1 daughter Margretlin.

75. Peter *Jung*, wool-weaver, Engel, 1 son Johannes, 1 daughter Katereinichen, master-workman Hans *Metzger* of Stegen.

76. Philips *Haupert*, wool-weaver, Agnes, 1 daughter Margretichen, apprentice Nickel Clas.

77. Hans *Herter*, wool-weaver, Barbel, 1 son Johannes, 3 daughters: Margreta, Ketichen, Sibilla.

78. Hans *Streckseisen*, blacksmith, Anna, 4 sons: Hans, Johannes, Jost, Hans Wiltz, 2 daughters: Barbel, Margreta.

79. Jacob *Müller*, baker, Els, 3 sons: Hans Peter, Johans, Hans Philips, 1 daughter: Ketereinichen.

80. Hans *Moch*, innkeeper, Petronella, 2 sons: Jörg Albrecht, Hans Heinrich, 3 daughters: Elisabeth, Anna Margret, Maria Magdalena.

81. Peter *Spitz*, tanner, Katharina.

82. Abraham *Becker*, baker, Martha.

83. Abrahams Junghans *Beckers*, baker, Margreta, 1 son Johanneslin, female servant: Agnes, Daniels Margret daughter of Cussel.

84. Bernhart *Debolt*, shoemaker, Katharina, 2 daughters: Margretichen, Martha.

85. Simon *Weber*, wool-weaver, Katharina.

86. Johannes *Gros*, wool-weaver, Elisabeth, 3 daughters: Margreta, Anna Maria, Anna Elisabeth, male servant: Peter Gros, Nicklas, Heinrich Polen's son of Niderlands, female servant: Anna, Götter Heinrich's daughter of Achtelsbach.

87. Jacob *Schlos*, weaver, Katharina, 1 son Johannes, 3 daughters: Barbichen, Mareylin, Gretichen.

88. *Koch* Hans, farmer, Margreta, 2 daughters: Barbichen, Eufrosyne.

f. 162

89. Michel *Faist*, tanner, Clara, 3 sons: Peter, Jörg, Johanneslin, 1 daughter Margreta, male servant: Clas of Oberkirchen, female sarvant Anna of Schwarzerd.

90. Philips *Wolf*, innkeeper, Margreta, 3 sons: Abraham, Hans Isaac, Hans Jacob, 1 daughter: Maria Salome, female servant: Maria of Gimpfweiler.

91. Johan *Gimbsbach*, Martha, 1 son Hans Jacob, 1 daughter Katharein.

92. Hans *Raut*, baker and shopkeeper, Katharina, 3 sons: Hans Nickel, Hans Jacob, Hans Abraham, female servant: Elisabeth of the Lutzelberger district.

93. Hans *Mair*, tawer, Els, 5 sons: Johannes, Hans Peter, Hans Nickel, Hans Martin, Hans Abraham, 1 daughter Maria.

94. Wilhelm *Doll*, day-labourer, Agnes, 2 daughters, Eufrosyne, Gretichen.
95. Nickel *Sailer*, hatmaker, Christina, 1 son: Hans Nickel.
96. Hans *Becker*, shopkeeper, Barbara, 2 sons: Peter, Hans Daniel, 1 daughter Ketichen.
97. Peter *Gerlach*, shoemaker, Barbara, 1 son Hans Debolt, 2 daughters: Margretichen, Ketichen.
98. Bartel *Schwott*, blacksmith, Barbel, 1 son, Johannislin, 2 daughters: Mareylin, Barbelichen.
99. Jacob *Popp*, wool-weaver, Anna, 1 son Conrad, 2 daughters: Anna Mädichen, Agneslin.
100. Hans *Clas*, innkeeper, Margreta, 2 daughters: Barbel and Ketichen.
101. Johannes *Schwab*, wool-weaver, Katharina, 1 son Johannes, 3 daughters: Maria, Els, Brigitta.

1. Clara (!) *Simon*, widower ⎫ these have neither chil-
2. Nickel *Zehend*, widower ⎪ dren nor other servants
3. Alt Hans *schmid*, widower ⎬ with them and live in
4. Peter *Achtelsbacher*, ⎪ the house of their chil-
   widower ⎭ dren or grandchildren.
5. Hans *Doll* the older, tailor, a widower, lives with his son Hans.
6. Wendel *Gall*, widower, daughter Madlena.
7. Nickel *Kümel*, wool-weaver, widower, 3 sons: Hans Jacob, Hans Enoch, Hans Nickel, 1 daughter Anna Margreta, male servants: Hans and Remig, Italians (''welsche''), Els an Italian female servant.
8. Johannes *Knoll*, salt-measurer, daughter: Särichen.

20 Widows:

1. Maria *Schwotin*, female servant, Els, Hans Lawer's daughter of Hiffeler.
2. Varina, Märtin *Seckler's* widow, lives with her daughter Katharina, Hans Rauten's (wife).
3. *Polands* Apell, is in the house of her son-in-law Weigand *Hederich*, tailor.
4. Elisabeth *Gossenbergerin*, 1 son Hans Simon, 2 daughters: Katharein, Anna Maria.
5. Margreta, *Bruder* Hansen's widow, 3 sons: Jost, Johannies, Hans Veltin, 2 daughters: Margreta, Madlena.
6. Katharin, Hans *Heckman's* widow, 1 son Hanse.
7. Särichen, Peter *Fläschen's* widow, with her son-in-law Michel Zimmerman.
8. Margreta, Daniel *Clunten* widow, 1 son Hans Jacob, daught. Barbel.
9. Katharin, Tobias *Weiganden's* widow, 1 son Hans Conrad.
10. Margreta, Balthas *Braunen's* (widow).
11. Margreta, Hans *Adam's* (widow).
12. Katharina, Stoffel *Müller's* (widow).

13. *Seitzen's* Katerin, 2 sons: Hans, a linen-weaver, Peter, who is called the blind Peter.

f. 163 14. Maria, Hans *Zen's* widow, potter, 2 sons: Theis, Hans Peter, 1 daughter Elisabetichen, potter's servant Wolf.

15. Apell *Trichtingerin*, 2 sons: Nickel, Stoffel.

16. Katharin, Peter *Knollen* widow, 1 son Nickel, 1 daughter Anna Maria.

17. *Clesichen's* Katharin.

18. *Schweitzer's* Katharein.

19. *Saw* Sarichen.

20. Madlena, Johann *Hofman's* widow, 2 sons: Hans Friederich, Hans Daniel, 1 daughter Anna Margreta, female servant Katharina Opin widow.

> 567 persons in all.

f. 163 c. List of the inhabitants of the parish *Cussel* and the villages and boroughs belonging to this parish.

Blaubach.[1]

1. Simon *Jung*, censor, Varina, son Antonius, female servants: Barbel, Kuehansen's daughter in the valley of Liechtenberg.

2. Jacob *Bair*, farmer, Maria, 1 son Hans, 4 daughters: Barbel, Keterin, Madlenichen, Elsichen.

3. Clas *Jung*, linen-weaver, Katharin, 1 son Nickel, 2 daughters: Margretichen, Martha.

4. Valentin *Fueger*, linen-weaver, Margreta, 1 son Jonas, 5 daughters: Barbichen, Kathereinichen, Apollonia, Margretlin, Elsichen.

5. Heintzen *Daniel*, butcher, Margreta, male servant: Hanse.

6. Thomas *Hirt*, shepherd, Margreta, shepherd's boy Hensichen.

7. Jacob *Leiddich*, farmer, Els, 1 son Hans, 1 daughter Margretlein.

8. Clas *Baur*, farmer, Margret, 2 daughters: Sibilla, Sara, male servant: Hans Jacob, a poor orphan.

9. Johannes *Runck*, farmer, Katharin, 3 sons: Jacobichen, Johanneslin, Simon.

Two Widows:

1. *Schneider's* Els, Maria, vidua, hujus ancilla.

2. Els, *Naw Nickel's* widow.

> Summa: 9 married couples, 2 widows, 8 sons, 14 daughters, 3 male servants, 2 female servants.

---

[1] North of Kusel.

Diedelkopf.[1]

f. 164.

1. Abraham *Jung*, censor, Sibilla, 3 sons: Abraham, Johannes, Clas, male servant: Hans App.
2. Simon *Hawden Span*, beadle of Pfeffelbach, **Margreta**, 1 son Junghans.
3. Simon *Heilman*, thatcher, Els, 1 son Nickel.
4. Simon *Queck*, farmer, Agnes, 2 sons: Abraham, Debolt.
5. Abraham *Queck*, farmer, Katharin.
6. Johannes *Lawer*, day-labourer, Christina, 1 son Hans Peter, 3 daughters: Agnes, Margret, Els.
7. Wilhelm *Stroschneider*, straw-cutter, Margreta.
8. Simon *Kramp*, farmer, Sara, 2 daughters, Apell, Maria.
9. Nickel *Seupt*, day-labourer, Katherin, 1 son Johannes, 4 daughters: Salome, Els, Katharin, Apollonia.
10. Hans *Bollenbacher*, butcher, Katharin, 1 son Andreas.
11. Hans *Bueb*, tailor, Engel, 3 daughters: Katharein, Els, Agnes.
12. Noe *Müller*, miller, Apollonia, 4 sons: Johannes, Debolt, Abraham, Johannes, 4 daughters: Maria, Barbel, Madlena, Kunigund.
13. Clas *Schäffer*, shepherd, Madlena, 1 son Johannes, 2 daughters Engel, Martha.
14. Haman *Bueb*, shoemaker, Katharin, 2 daughters: Agnes, Margreta.
15. Bastian *Jung*, farmer, Madlena, 2 sons Nickel, Johannes.
16. Conrad *Clas*, peasant, Margreta, 1 son: Nickelichen.
17. Hans *Knap*, day-labourer, Margreta.

Hans *Flieg*, cooper, widower, 5 daughters: Christina, Madlena, Katharein, Anna Gretichen, Mareylin.

Sara Debolt *Bueben's* widow, 2 children: Bastian, Els.

Margreta, *Jung* Hansen widow, is in the house of her son Abraham Jung.

Margreta, *Hirt* Bastian's widow.

Müller Barbel (widow).

Blödesbach.[2]

1. Hans *Jung*, censor Barbel, male servant: Johannes of Oberkirchen.
2. *Acker* Hans, farmer, Katharein, 4 sons: Johannes, Hans, Jacob, Nickel.
3. *Matthes* Nickel, farmer, Margareth, 4 sons: Simon, Johannes, Abraham, Nickel, 2 daughters: Maria, Annichen.
4. Abraham *Baur*, farmer, Apell, son: Simon, 3 daughters: Margreta, Barbel, Margretichen.
5. Jacob *Jung*, farmer, Katharein, 3 sons: Johannes, Hans, Hans(?), 1 daughter: Margreta.

---

[1] Northwest of Kusel, on the road to Thallichtenberg.

[2] Bledesbach, southwest of Kusel.

6. Matthes *Teis*, farmer, Anna, 3 sons: Johannes, Hans Tobias, Hans Adam, 3 daughters: Elsichen, Sinichen, Ketereinichen.

7. *Fridel* sine cognomine(!), shepherd, Margreta, daughter: Klein Els.

8. Nickel *Klein*, farmer, Katharein, 2 sons: Hans Nickel, Junghans, 2 daughters: Elsichen, Engelichen.

9. Daniel *Hirt*, shepherd, Otilia, 1 son Hans Nickel, 2 daughters: Katereinichen, Annichen.

10. Hans *Müller*, miller, Maria, son: Adam, studiosus, 1 daughter: Kathareinichen.

11. Johannes *Müller*, miller, Katharina, 2 sons: Hans and Hans Adam.

12. *Welsch* Hans, brick-layer, Katharina, 3 sons: Hans, Conrad, Wilhelm, 3 daughters: Kathareinichen, Annichen, Margretichen, male servant: Hans.

13. Hans *Stroschneider*, widower, a straw-cutter.

14. Katharina, *Clasen* Simon's widow.

Eheweiler.

f. 165

1. Bastian *Peters*, censor, Agnes, 1 son Hans, 2 daughters: Barbel, Katharein.

2. Hans *Hinterer* vulgo Fuhrhans, day-labourer, Maria.

3. David *Stroschneider*, farmer, Katharin, 3 sons: Bastian, Abrahamichen, Jünghans, 1 daughter Margreta.

4. Abraham *Heilman*, linen-weaver, Margreta, 2 sons: Bastian, Bartelin, 2 daughters: Agnes, Elsichen.

5. Hans *Peter*, farmer, Els, daughter: Margreta.

6. Bartel, Hans *Peter's* son, day-labourer, Sibilla.

7. Johannes *Kickel*, farmer, Agnes, 1 son Nickelchen, 2 daughters Margretichen, Kathareinichen.

8. Johannes, *Peters* Hansen son, day-labourer, Francisca.

9. Hans *Hennessen*, farmer, Barbel, 1 son Wilhelm, 1 daughter Margreta, male servant: Nickel Knaur of Schwarzerden.

f. 165 v.

10. Johannes *Turn*, farmer, Sibilla, 1 son Junghans, 3 daughters: Sara, Keterichen, Barbel.

11. Clas *Veltin*, straw-cutter, and farmer, Katharein, 1 son Bastian, 4 daughters, Johanna, Sibilla, Margreta, Katharin.

12. *Schwartz* Hans, shepherd, Gertraut, male servant, Mathes, Veltin Fueger's son of Blaubach.

13. Johanna, David, *Martin's* widow.

14. Katharin, Bartel *Kleinen* widow, 2 sons: Jung Hans, Bastian.

Wanwegen.

1. Simon *Koch*, censor, Adelheid, male servant Martin Pfeiffer; female servant: Margreta, Debolt Koch's daughter, an orphan.

2. Abraham *Ziegler*, tiler, Otilia, 1 son Hensichen, 2 daughters: Christina, Margreta.
3. Hans *Tholer*, brick-layer, Gertrud, 2 sons: Clas, Peter, 3 daughters: Margreta, Annichen, Agneslın.
4. Nickel *Naw*, brick-layer, Anna, 3 sons, Hans Wendel, Nickel, Wilhelmichen, 3 daughters: Els, Egnes, Martha.
5. Matthes N., wool-weaver, Anna, 1 son Hans Daniel.
6. *Jung Hansens* Bartel, day-labourer, Els, 1 daughter Appolonia.
7. *Niclas* Hans, farmer, Els, 1 son, 1 daughter Elsichen.
8. *Klein* Hans, peasant, Katharina, 5 sons: Hans, Hänsichen, Adam, Nickelichen, Johannichen.

f. 166
9. Nickel *Kramp*, peasant, Els, 4 sons: Jacob, Hanse, Nickel, Hensichen, 5 daughters: Agnes, Engel, Maria, Margreta, Walburg.
10. Hans *Haut*, peasant, Katharina, 1 son Abraham, 2 daughters Martha, Els.
11. Hans *Seupert*, day-labourer, Otilia, 2 sons: Johanneslin, Hans Jacobichen, male servant: Stoffel.
12. *Bartel* Hans, peasant, Otilia, 2 sons: Nickel and Hensichen, 2 daughters: Adelheid, Martha.
13. Johan *Sawheil*, swineherd, Els.
14. Adam *Koch*, cowherd, Agnes.
15. Hans *Schäffer*, shepherd, Adelheit, 2 daughters: Elsichen, Adelheid, shepherd's servant: Bastian.
16. Katharina, *Junghansen's* widow.
17. Maria, Debolt *Geiger's* widow.

Hiffelers and Rentzweiler.[1]

1. Abraham *Klunt*, censor, Els.
2. Nickel *Jung*, censor, Katharein, 1 son Hans.
3. Nickel *Mair*, juror, Martha, 3 sons: Peter, Nickel, Johannes, 2 daughters: Margretlin, Elsichen.
4. Clas *Rentzweiler*, peasant, Els, 1 son, Abraham, 1 daughter Els.
5. Martin *Stroschneider*, peasant, Barbel, 2 daughters.
6. Hans *Lawer*, linen-weaver, Barbel, 1 son Johannes, 2 daughters: Katharina, Otilia.

f. 166 v.
7. Elsen Hans (*Staud*), peasant, Maria, 3 sons: Debolt, Abraham, Klein Hans, 2 daughters: Elisabeth, Martha.
8. Adam *Schneider*, peasant, Els, 1 son Bartel, 1 daughter Barbel.
9. Hans *Kercher*, peasant, Agnes.
10. Nickel *Kercher*, peasant, Apollonia, 4 sons: Nickel, Hans, Adam, Johanneslin, 2 daughters: Agnes, Adelheit.
11. Remig *Müller*, peasant, Els: 1 son: Hans, 2 daughters: Marey, Clärichen.

---

[1] Küffler, southeast of Konken.

12. Hans *Schmidt*, blacksmith, Maria, 2 sons: Nickel, Niclesichen, 2 daughters: Katharein, Apell.
13. *Debolts* Hans, peasant, Maria.
14. *Debolts* Hansen, Simon, peasant, Barbara, 6 sons: Nickel, Debold, Clerichen, Bartel, Petichen, Simon, 2 daughters: Margreta, Els.
15. Barthel *Koch*, butcher, Sibilla, 1 son Adam.
16. *Debolt* Jörg, Bartel Kochsaiden, straw-cutter, Agnes, 1 son: Hänsichen, 1 daughter Elsichen.
17. *Wendels* Hans, peasant, Kätterin, 1 son Hans, 1 female servant: Elsichen.
18. Katharina, *Klein* Hansen's widow, 1 son Hans, 1 daughter.

Schelweiler.[1]

1. Remig *Jung*, peasant, Margreta, 1 son: Hans Pirmin, 2 daughters: Kathareinchen, Annichen, 2 male servants: Jonas of Pfeffelbach, Hans, Elsen Hansen's (Staud) son of Hiffelers.
2. Hans *Thomas*, shepherd, Margreta, 1 son Abraham, 2 daughters: Margreta, Barbalichen.

3. *Remigs* Adam, peasant, Barbel; she has left him recently and is said to stay somewhere in the country; 3 sons: Debolt, Peter, Adam, 2 daughters: Margretlin, Barbichen, whom the woman has taken along.
4. Hans *Naw*, day-labourer, Margreta, 2 sons: Jost, Hans, 1 daughter: Els.
5. Michel *Zimmermann*, carpenter, Anna, 1 daughter Annichen.
6. Maister Hans *Debolt*, farmer, Margreta, 1 son Johannes.
7. Adam *Zimmerman*, carpenter, Barbel, 4 sons: Hans Debolt, Hans, Adam, Hans Nickel, 1 daughter: Margreta, carpenter's boy: Veltin.
8. Bernhart *Clas*, day-labourer, Els, 2 sons: Franz, Peter.
9. Johann *Schwenck*, farmer, Margreta, 2 sons: David, Remig, 2 daughters: Elsabeth, Katharein.
10. Abraham *Jung*, peasant, Els, 3 sons: Nickel, Hans Nickel, Lorenz, 3 daughters: Margreta, Els, Barbel.
11. Franz *Zimmerman*, carpenter, Katharin, 1 son Hans Stoffel, 2 daughters: Madlena, Els.
12. Lorenz *Müller*, carpenter, Margreta, 1 son: Hans Remig, 2 daughters: Margreta, Elsichen.
13. Nickel *Lawer*, farmer, Barbel, 1 daughter: Barbel.
14. Johan *Morgenstern*, wool-weaver, Barbel, 2 male servants: Nickel of Wanwegen, Hans Nickel Mair of Cussel.
15. Hans *Schäffer*, shepherd, Johannat, 1 son: Hans Wilhelm, 1 daughter Els.

---

[1] Schellweiler, east of Konken.

16. Hans *Jung*, censor, widower, 2 sons: Abraham and Hans, 3 daughters: Els, Katharin, Klein Katharin.
17. Katharina, Debolt *Jungen's* widow, 1 son: Hans.
18. Madlena, Peter *Nickel's* widow.

f. 167 v.   *Etzberg*.[1]

1. Johannes *Schuchmacher*, censor, Katharina, 6 sons: Johannes, Bernhart, Barthel, Hans, Nickel, Kleinhans, female servant: Agnes.
2. Hensel *Schuchmacher*, peasant, Margreta, male servant Hans Kramp, female servant: Gertraut.
3. Johannes *Bösharen*, blacksmith, Katharina, 1 son Bernhart.
4. Johannes *Kramp*, butcher, Margreta, 2 sons: Junghans, Hans Debolt, 4 daughters: Margreta, Apollonia, Barbichen, Margretichen.
5. Hans *Külpich*, brick-layer, Els, 2 grandchildren: Margreta, Barbichen.
6. Johannes *Keiser*, butcher, Margreta, 1 son Hans Debolt.
7. Hans *Fuchs*, brick-layer, Margreta.
8. Debolt *Kesler*, brazier, Madlena.
9. Peter *Gartner*, gardener, Susanna, 1 son: Hans Bernhart, 2 daughters: Gretichen, Anna Margretichen.
10. Hans *Schumacher*, shoemaker, Maria, 1 daughter: Lisabetlin.
11. Debolt, flayer, Katharina.
12. Katharina, *Contzen* Debolt's widow.

f. 168   *Eisenbach* [2] on the Glan, above Gimbsbach.

1. David *Göltzenleuchter*, censor, Margreta, grandchild: Margreta, male servant: Johannes of Birsborn, female servant: Katharin Müller, Jacob's daughter of Rutweiler.
2. Johann, David *Göltzenleuchter's* son, farmer, Katharina, 2 sons: Joannes, Abraham, 1 daughter: Engel.
3. Johan *Mair*, farmer, Margreta, 2 daughters: Ketter, Annichen.
4. Debold *Schneider*, farmer, Els, 2 sons: Clas, Hans.
5. Nickel *Hafner*, wool-weaver, Sara, 2 daughters: Barbel, Els, male servant: Hans from Lotringen.
6. *Peters* Hans, farmer, Margreta, 2 sons, Clas, Hans, 2 daughters: Els, Katterichen.
7. Wilhelm *Hesel*, wool-weaver, Barbel, 2 sons: Thomas, Antoni, 1 daughter: Margreta, male servant: Simon *Staud* of Bosenbach, Gabriel Sorg of Müllenbach.
8. Philips *Niderländer*, wool-weaver, Els, 1 son Haupert, 1 daughter: Agnes, male serv. Schäffer Hans of Godelhaus.

---

[1] Etschberg, south of Kusel and east of Konken.
[2] Southeast of Kusel and Konken.

9. Hans *Clas*, linen-weaver, Getza, 1 son Johannes, 1 daughter: Margretlin.
10. Clas *Schuchmacher*, shoemaker, Margreta, 2 sons, Philips, Wendel, 1 daughter Elisabeth.
11. Clas *Jerusalem*, wool-weaver, Engel, 1 son Hans Henrich, 1 daughter Agnes.
12. Hans *Hirt*, cowherd, Christine.
13. Katharina, *Schäffer* Wendel's widow.

f. 168 v.   *Godelhausen.*[1]

1. Andres *Haintz*, censor, Margreta, 1 son Johannes, 1 grandchild: Agnes.
2. Johannes Henrich *Koch*, censor, Clara, 4 sons: Hans, Johannes, Jacob, Debolt, 1 daughter: Sara.
3. Noë *Scherer*, shearer, Clara.
4. Hans *Becker*, baker, Margreta.
5. *Junck* Hans, farmer, Ketterein, 1 daughter: Margreta.
6. Jacob, *Junck*—Hansen's son, farmer, Katharina, 1 daughter: Margretlin.
7. Debolt *Schlos*, miller, Agnes, 2 sons: Johannes, Nickel, 5 daughters: Eva, Apell, Barbel, Margreta, Katharin.
8. Debolt *Reutz*, joiner, Margreta, 1 daughter: Margretichen, male servant Debolt, joiner's boy Johannes.
9. Hans *Emerich*, Margreta, 3 sons: Johannes, Daniel, Hans Jacob, 2 daughters: Katharin, Elsichen.
10. Hans *Wendel*, farmer, Barbel, 1 son Johannes, 1 grandchild Nickel, 1 daughter, Geza.
11. Johan *Schneider*, tailor, Katharin.
12. Matthes *Ferg*, glazier, Barbel.
13. Remig *Fischer*, butcher, widower.
14. *Schneider's* Katharin, widow.
15. Valentin *Hirt*, shepherd, Martha, 1 son: Conrad.

f. 169   *Rammelsbach.*[2]

1. Debolt *Hofman*, censor, Margreta, 4 daughters: Margretichen, Sarichen, Agnes, Kathareinichen, male servant: Debolt.
2. Paulus *Förg*, thatcher, Martha.
3. Nickel *Lawer*, farmer, Maria, 3 sons: Hans, Debolt, Hans Nickel, 1 daughter: Margreta.
4. Hans *Rausch*, day-labourer, Margreta.
5. Stoffel *Arnold*, farmer and innkeeper, Sibilla, 1 son: Johannes, 2 daughters: Sara and Margreta.
6. Hans *Müller*, farmer, Apollonia.
7. Klein Katharein, *Jung* Debolt's widow.

---

[1] Southeast of Kusel.

[2] Rammelsbach, east of Kusel.

[Until recently the manuscript ended here; the following pages were missing and could not be traced in spite of numerous inquiries in the competent parishes. Even repeated and careful examinations of the archives in the rectory of Konken had no success.

From the composition of the manuscript it could be seen that the missing part contained the parish of Niederkirchen in the Osterthal ("Easter Valley") with the boroughs of Bubach, Marth, Saal, Leitersweiler, Crugelborn zum Hoof, Osterbrücken and Selchenbach, also the parish of Quirnbach with Reichartsweiler, Rehweiler, Liebsthal, Trahweiler and Frutzweiler. I therefore decided to speak to the clergyman of Niederkirchen and traveled to the Osterthal late in the fall of 1924. This time all corners coming into consideration were searched thoroughly and the sheets were found.

It may be supposed that a couple of years ago a clergyman of Niederkirchen removed these sheets from the volume and took them along, as they interested him especially. Meanwhile he died, and the manuscript thus remained unknown and unnoticed in his archives. Now, it has been correctly replaced in the book.—HERM. FRIEDR. MACCO.]

Nr. 45
f. 182/2   List of the annual competency and income that is paid and delivered truly and approximately to a clergyman of Niederkirchen, noted on May 22nd, anno 1609.

f. 183   Nota. A list of all married couples, children and servants
Nr. 46   of each village of the parish of Niederkirchen, on May 22nd, anno 1609, during the church visitations, registered by me, Wolfgango Herters, ministro indigno of this place.

f. 184   *Married couples of Niderkirchen,* 40 persons in all:

1. Wolfgang *Herter*, clergyman, his wife Katharina.
2. Johann *Neufardt*, schoolmaster, his wife Margret, daughters: Anna and Sara.
3. Jacob *Seiler*, church-jurat, his wife Margret, son: Johannes.
4. *Seiler's* Nickel, his wife Margret, children: Hans, Nickel and Johannes.
5. *Weil* Moses, linen-weaver and his wife Demut, son: Melchior.
6. *Culman*, his wife Christina, children: Jacob, Maria, Agnes and Catharina.
7. *Keller* Hans, his wife Barbel, children Johannes, Hans Jacob, Els, Appolonia.
8. *Trantz*, cowherd, his wife Margret, daughter: Christina.
9. *Schneider* Johannes, his wife Els, children: Adam, Johannes and Margret.
10. Remmen *Metzler*, his wife Margret.
11. Adam *Becker*, his wife Katharina, children: Johannes, Adam, Nickel, Barbel & Christina.

12. Endres *Geiger*, his wife Agnes, son: Baschen.
13. *Beckers* Nickel, his wife Agnes, children: Johannes, Katharina, Margreta.
14. *Kühe* Hans, his wife Barbel.
15. Marx *Zimmermann*, his wife Christine, son: Simon.
16. Hans *Huttmacher*, his wife Margret, children: Adam and Margreta.
17. Hans *Klein*, wheelwright, his wife Agnes.
18. *Hüel* Nickel, his wife Engel, children: Johannes, Haupert, Hensgen, Anna, Barbel.
19. *Gerten* Hans, his wife Appolonia, son: Hans Nickel.
20. Hans *Müller* in den Dieffenbach, his wife Maria, children: Hans Jacob, Els, Maria and Appolonia.

Children of the parish of Niderkirchen:

Glöckners Johannes children: Hans Jacob, Diebolt and Agnes.
Bender Elsen children: Margret and Agnes.

6 widowed persons of the parish of Niederkirchen:

1. *Glöckner* Johannes.
2. *Melchiors* Ketter.
3. *Gerten* Johannes.
4. *Weil* Agnes.
5. *Bender* Els.
6. *Hüel* Gert.

Servants, 6 persons in all:

Agnes, the clergyman's female servant.
Melchior, *Weyl* Moses' male servant.
Mattes, Adam *Becker's* male servant.
Johannes, the *hatmaker's* male servant.
Hans *Kleinen's* male servant Johannes.
Catharina, his female servant.
Summa of all old and young persons in the parish of Niderkirchen, 97.

f. 184 v.   *Married couples in the parish of Mahrt*, 26 persons in all:

1. Peter *Becker*, his wife Margret, children: Johannes, Jochim, Els and Metz.
2. Bachen *Zimmerman*, his wife Engel, children: Johannes and Jacob.
3. Johann *Schmidt*, his wife Catharina.
4. *Schöflers* Diebolt, his wife Margret, children: Christina, Margret, Agnes and Johannes.
5. Simon *Geltzlichter*, his wife Maria, child: Niklas.
6. *Weil* Michel der schöffer, his wife Margret, children: Johannes and Catharina.
7. Thomas *Bruch*, cowherd, his wife Barbel, son: Hans Jacob.

8. *Schneider* Hans, his wife Barbel, children: Hans Jacob, Hans Adam, Wendel, Engel.
9. Jacob *Schuemacher*, his wife Catharina, children: Jacob, Wendel, Johannes, Margret, Barbel, Engel.
10. Franz *Müller*, his wife Margret, children: Jacob, Cornelius, Barbel, Christina and Els.
11. *Höhe* Jacob, his wife Agnes, children: Agnes and Ketterin.
12. *Höhe* Baschen, his wife Margret.
13. Hans *Wagner* of Wurschweiler uf dem hoff, and his wife Eva, children: Melchior, Cornelius, Niclas, Hans Adam, Johannes, Els, Agnes, Margret and Katterein.

Children at Mahrt, 44 in all:

Weissgerbers Althansen' sons: Adam, Johannes and Niklas.
Schmidts Althansen son: Johannes, a tailor.

Servants at Mahrt, 4 in all.

Peter *Becker's* male servant Hans Wolf.
Althansen fem. servant Ketter(in) who came from Busen.
Baschen *Zimmerman's* male servant Adam.
Jacob *Schuemacher's* male servant Jacob.

Widowed persons at Mahrt, 2 in all:

Althans *Weisgerber*.
Christina, *Schmidt's* Althansen widow.

Sum of old and young persons in the parish of Mahrt, 76 in all.

f. 185   *Married couples in the parish zum Saal.*

1. *Laus* Adam, his wife Appolonia, children: Adam and Johannes.
2. Hans *Seiler*, his wife Margret, child: Barbel.
3. Nickel *Seiler*, his wife Catharina, children: Hans Jacob, Johannes, Theis, David, Conrad, Agnes and Margret.
4. Theis *Schuemacher*, his wife Margret, child: Hans Jacob.
5. Hans *Reutter*, his wife Agnes, children: Margret and Katterein.
6. *Lawer* Jacob, his wife Christina, children: Christina, Ketterein, Appolonia and Moyses.
7. *Zimmer* Hans, his wife Katharina, children: Engel and Appolonia.
8. Philipp and his wife Margret, children: Melchior, Appolonia.
9. Diebolt *Steinmetz*, his wife Engel, children, Pette, Agnes, Catharina, Klein Ketter, Johannes and Melchior.
10. *Kaden* Michel and his wife Maria.
11. *Jung* Hans, his wife Catharina.

12. Michel *Müller*, his wife Engel, children: Johannes, Hans
Adam, Catharina and Christina.

Children zum Saal: 35 in all.

Schärte's Agnesen children: Gertraud and Margreta.

Vidua: *Schärte's* Agnes.

Sum of old and young persons in the parish zum Saal,
60 in all.

f. 185 v.   *Married couples in the parish of Bubach,* 32 persons in all.

1. *Zimmer* Diebolt, his wife Engel, children: Margret,
Metz and Barbel.
2. *Stro* Diebolt, linen-weaver, his wife Margret, children:
Christina, Niklas and Hans Diebolt.
3. *Gärtners* Johannes, his wife Ketter, daughters: Barbel
and Agnes.
4. Gall *Lawer*, his wife Amelia, children: Margret, Gertraud and Simon.
5. Peter *Schmidt*, his wife Barbel, children: Margret, Su-
sann, Appolonia, Johannes, Sebastian, Hensgen, Hans
Nickel, Hans Philipp and Niclas.
6. Johannes *Klein*, a tanner, his wife Metz, children:
Peter and Agnes.
7. *Weber* Adam, his wife Margret, children: Johannes and
Katterein.
8. *Moyses*, a church-jurat, his wife Ketterein, children:
Johannes and Margret.
9. *Metzlers* Diel, his wife Maria, children: Moyses, Hans
Diebolt, Agnes.
10. The young *Moyses*, a thatcher, his wife Marget, children: Maria, Katharina.
11. *Laux* the juror, his wife Ketter.
12. *Görg Schmidt*, his wife Ketter.
13. *Zimmer* Hans, his wife Söntgen, children: Johannes,
Katharina and Agnes.
14. Albrecht *Pulvermacher*, his wife Agnes, children: Baschen, Heinrich and Hans Jacob.
15. Adam *Zimmerman*, his wife Margret, child: Anna
Christina.
16. *Sixt* the cowherd, his wife Els, children: Johannes and
Hensgen.

Viduae, 6 widowed persons:

1. *Stro* Barbel, children: Appel, Agnes and Niclas.
2. *Metzel* Barbel, children: Johannes, Ketterein, Hensgen.
3. *Schneiders* Agnes.
4. *Ottilia,* the juror's mother.
5. *Schöffer* Adam, viduus.
6. Söntgen, *Metzel* Dielen' mother.

Sum of old and young persons in the parish of Bubach,
87 in all.

f. 186   *Married couples in the parish of Leuttersweiler.*

1. Nickel *Müller*, mayor, his wife Els, children: Johannes, Lucas, Maria and Catharina.
2. *Schöflers* Diebolt, his wife Els, children: Adam, Johannes, Niklas, Agnes, Katharina, Margret, Maria Appolonia.
3. Nickel *Lang*, his wife Katharina, children: Johannes, Niclas, Appolonia, Els, Eva, Christina.
4. *Schneider* Hans, his wife Katharina, son: Johannes.
5. Hans *Lang*, tailor, his wife Anna, children: Johannes, Els and Martin.
6. *Wagners* Hans, his wife Margret, children: Culman and Appolonia.
7. *Lang* Michel, his wife Agnes, children: Johannes, Nic [*sic*] scholar Hans, Cornelius, Engel.
8. Nickel *Weisgerber*, his wife Maria, children: Christina, Agnes and Katharina.
9. Görg *Steinmetz*, his wife Margret, children: Hans Nickel, Diebolt, Johannes, Christina.
10. Nesen *Wendel*, his wife Catharina, children:
11. *Steupers* Nickel, his wife Christina, children: Margret, Agnes, Barbel, Ketterein, Christine, Johannes.
12. *Josten* Nickel the shepherd, his wife Margret, children: Els, Wendel, Hans Nickel.
13. *Steupers* Junghans, his wife Barbel.
14. Christman *Eick*, linen-weaver, his wife Ketterein, daughter: Agnes.
15. *Jochims* Hans, his wife Agnes.
16. *Metzel* Klas, his wife Agnes.
17. Nickel *Metzler*, his wife Ketter.
18. Hans *Becker*, a juror of the court of Hoff, his wife Margret, children: Johannes, Niklas and Maria.
19. *Joachim*, a church jurat, his wife Appolonia.

Sum, 38 persons, 51 children.

Servants:

Joachim's Hansen 2 male servants, Diebolt, Johannes, his female servant Els.
Hans *Becker's* male servant Hans, his fem. serv. Ketter.

Widows: Wagner's Agnes.

Sum of old and young persons in the parish of Leuttersweiler, 95 in all.

f. 186 v.   *Married couples of half the parish of Crugelborn.*

1. *Schweitzer* Hans, a ''rödler'', his wife Elisabeth, children: Johannes, Elisabeth, Esther, Froneka.
2. *Isaac*, a ''rödler'', his wife Adelheid, children: Sara, Magdalena.

3. *Dielen* Jacob, his wife Margret, children: Johannes, Niclas, Cornelius, Christman, Veltin, Anna, Maria, Appolonia and Katharina.
4. *Schaden* Hans, his wife Anna, children: Matthes, Christman, Maria, Margret.
5. Hans *Hartman*, his wife Anna.
6. *Alles* Nickel, his wife Dathein, son: Johannes.
7. *Alles* Wendel, his wife Aell, children: Johannes, Christman, Niklas, Els, Christina, Maria.

Summa, 14 persons, 25 children.

Widows: 3 persons:

Niklas *Schneider, Lawers* Els, Maria *Friesin.*

Sum of persons who belong to the half parish of Crugelborn and our parish-church of Niederkirchen,—42 in all.

f. 187

Married couples of the parish zum Hoff, 36 persons 48 children:

1. *Schmidts* Jacob, a censor and court-juror zum Hoff, his wife Christina, children: Adam, Johannes, Jacob, Hans Jacob, Margret, Agnes.
2. *Rottbarts* Gerlich, his wife Christina, children: Hans Michael, Barbel and Agnes.
3. *Schmidts* Michel, his wife Agnes, children: Agnes, Christina, Barbel and Adam.
4. Hans *Schüler,* his wife Engel, children: Christina, his brothers are Jacob and Kleinhans.
5. *Höwe* Nickel, his wife Eva, children: Hans Jacob, Agnes and Christina.
6. *Büttels* Adam, his wife Gertta, children: Johannes, Adam, Margret and Eva.
7. *Hellen* Michel, his wife Barbel, children: Johannes and Ketterein.
8. *Müel* Seimot, a miller, his wife Christina, children: Johannes and Eva.
9. Miller Seimot's son-in-law *Simon,* his wife Christina.
10. *Schöffer* Seimot, his wife Margret, children: Johannes, Christman, Els and Katharina.
11. *Seuberts* Hans and Barbel his wife, children: Adam, Hans Adam, Agnes, Margreta.
12. *Müel* Seimots Hans, his wife Margret, children: Adam, Simon, Michel and Katharina.
13. Hans *Wagner,* his wife Christina, children: Adam, Hans Michel and Barbel.
14. *Müller* Adam, his wife Barbel, children: Hans Jacob, Barbel, Margret.
15. Cornelius *Zimmerman,* his wife Katharina, son: Hans Jacob, grandchild: Johannes.
16. *Rotbarts* Michel, his wife Margret.
17. *Zimmer* Adam, his wife Anna, son Johannes.
18. *Christman* cowherd, his wife Agnes.

Servants: 4 persons.

Schüler's male servant: Hans Adam.
Hell Wendel's male servant: Diebolt.
Büttels Adam's female servant: Maria.
Hellen Michel's male servant: Diebolt.

Widower and widows: 3 persons.

Weisen Hans.
Ottilia.
Rottbarts Margret.

Sum of old and young persons of this parish, 91 in all.

f. 187 v.   *Married couples at Osterbrücken,* 28 persons, 51 children:

1. *Heinsel,* censor, viduus, children: Johannes, Jacob, Cornelius and Margret.
1. *Schneider* Jacob the old, his wife Maria, children: Johannes and Agnes.
2. *Schneider* Jacob the young, his son, his wife Els, children: Antonius, Els, Margret and Niklas.
3. *Schwartzen* Kläsgen, his wife Eva, children: Johannes, Jacob, Demut.
4. Wendel *Wagner,* his wife Margret, children: Jacob, Ketterein and Els.
5. *Philippen* Veit, his wife Dathein, children: Margret, Agnes, Maria and Demut.
6. Caspar *Zimmermann,* his wife Engel.
7. Klas *Zimmerman,* his wife Maria, children: Antonius, Jacob, Martin, Engel and Anna.
8. *Schneider* Hans, his wife Margret, children: Johannes, Engel, Ketter.
9. *Trumpel* Diebolt, his wife Catharina, children: Jacob, Wendel, Johannes, Cornelius, Niclas.
10. Kleinhans *Wagner,* his wife Ottilia.
11. *Kleinhansen* Nickel, his son, his wife Agnes, children: Michel, Engel, Agnes, Margret.
12. Heinrich *Schöffer,* his wife Els, children: Adam, Johannes, Katharina, Margret.
13. *Müller* Hans, his wife Engel, children: Johannes, Margret and Catharina.
14. *Müller* Jacob, his wife Margret, children: Johannes, Ketter and Els.

Widower and widows: 5 persons.

Heinsel, censor.
Schleidt Margret, children: Adam and Jacob.
Theisen Margret.
Theisen Barbel.
Johannet, the widow's daughters: Els and Ketter.

Sum of old and young persons: 84 in all.

---

* So in text.

f. 188   *Married couples at Selchenbach,* 22 persons.

1. Hans *Theisinger,* a church-jurat, his wife Els, children: Johannes, Niclas, Margret.
2. *Junghenn* Diebolt, his wife Ottilia.
3. *Appeln* Adam, a juror of the court of Cusseln, his wife Els, children: Diebolt, Niclas, Engel and Maria.
4. *Metzel* Diebolt, his wife Margret, children: Johannes, Hentsgen, Ottilia, Engel, Margret, Ketterein.
5. *Gros* Nickel, his wife Christina, children: Niclas, Els and Margret.
6. *Meyers* Diebolt, his wife Barbel, children: Niclas and Ketterein.
7. *Schneider* Hans, his wife Ketterein.
8. Hans *Morgenstern,* his wife Ketter, daughter: Els.
9. Hans *Bast,* his wife Margret, son: Niclas.
10. *Schöffer* Diebolt, his wife Maria, children: Velten, Remmen, Johannes, Margret, Katharina.
11. *Veitts* Diebolt, his wife Els, daughter: Jung Margret.
12. *Viduae,* 5 persons.
    Mergen Agnes.
    Appeln Hansen, Ketter.
    Theisen Kettern, the widow's children are: Junghans, Johannes, Margret and Agnes.
    Veitten Marien, the widow's children are: Johannes, Margret and Engel.
    Groshans.   Summa: 33 children.

    Servants: Christina, Mergen Agnesen, female servant Schneider Hansen, female servant *Peter.*

    Summa: 62 persons, all old and young people.

    Nota: Summa summarum of all married people in all villages—260 in all.
    Summa summarum of all children, young and older, of all villages—381 in all.
    Summa of all servants—21 in all.
    Summa summarum of all widowers and widows—32 persons in all.

    Nota: Sum of all people, married couples, children, servants, and widowers and widows—694 persons in all.

f. 194   List of all inhabitants in the parish of the Chapel of *Quirnbach* in the six villages:

1. Quirnbach,   4. Traweiller,
2. Reichardsweiler,   5. Frutzweiller,
3. Reheweiller,   6. Liebenstahl.

    Written down by me, the below-mentioned Johannen Helffenstein, ecclesiastem Conckanum, on May 18th, anno 1609.

f. 195   Nr. 49   *The Chapel of Quirnbach.*[1]

1. *Heilman,* linen-weaver, Brigitta, 6 children: Margret 14
   years, Theobald 12, Meckulda 10, Simon 8, Nickel 6,
   Otilia 2 years old.
2. *Cornelius,* wool-weaver, Barbara, 9 children: Maria 16
   years, Barbara 14, Christina 12, Anny 9, Agnes 7, Elisabeth 5, Johannes 4, Meckuldta 3, Wilhelm 2 years old.
3. Jacob *Creutz,* Margret, a young married couple, have no
   children yet.
4. Clos *Rindt,* Elisabeth, 4 children: Catharina 20 years,
   Barbara 18, Hanns 15, Bürtel 6 years.
5. Christina, Jonae *Rindten* widow, has five orphans:
   Elisabeth 20 years, Elias 9, Margret 12, Barbara 8, Johannes 7 years.

f. 195 v.   6. Hanns *Creutz,* Catharina, 7 children: Elisabeth 16 years,
   Engel 18, Johannes 13, Hans 10, Maria 7, Theobald 6,
   Catharina 4 years.
7. Theobald Georg, Barbara, 3 children: Johannes 20,
   Hanns 18, Catharina 16 years.
8. Simon *Schleich,* Maria, have her father Theobald Sleich
   with them, who is a widower, and they have 3 children:
   Tilleman 7, Jacob 5, Johannes 1½ years, who is blind
   ("diesem haben die purpeln beide augen ausgefressen").
9. Wolfgangus *Meyer,* (wife not named) have 2 children:
   Johannes 6, Appellonia 1½ years, 1 male servant Johannes of Eckersweiler, 1 female servant Meckel of
   Quirnbach.
10. Hanns *Matzenbach,* Barbara, no children, male servant
    Nickel of Ombach, fem. servant Catharina of Ombach.

f. 196   11. Johannes *Khühirt,* Maria, 3 children: Catharina 18,
    Simon 9, Elisabeth 4 years.
12. Nickel *Krämer,* Margret, 4 daughters: Anna 22, Me-
    chulda 18, Barbara 16, Maria 12 years.
13. Tielman *Reech,* Mechulda, 4 children: Kleinhanns 18,
    Elisabeth 16, Symon 12, Hanns Symon 10.
14. Johannes *Schneider,* Catharina, 2 children: Johannes 3,
    Barbara 2 years.
15. Johannes *Meyer,* Barbara, 5 children: Catharina 14,
    Engel 12, Peter 8, Jonas 7, Abraham 4 years.
16. Job *Weber,* viduus, has no children, 1 female servant.
17. Jonas *Weber,* Maria, have from both their former mar-
    riage 10 children: 1. Jonas' children: Daniel 18, Mar-
    gret 15, Martha 13, Magdalena 11, Catharina and Maria,
    twins, 9 years. 2. Marien' children: Hanns 16, Simon
    13, Tilman 11, Barbara 9 years.
18. Nickel *Heugell,* Elisabeth, 3 children: Elisabeth 7,
    Hanns 5, Catharina 8 weeks.

---

[1] South of Kusel.

19. Johannes *Schaffhirt*, Maria, 2 children: Johannes 1½ year, Anna Catharina 3 weeks.

f. 197 *The village of Reichartsweiler.*

1. Stefan *Weber*, Maria, 9 children: Agnes 17, Maria 15, Wendel 13, Lenhard 11, Margret 10, Barbara 7, Christa 5, Stefan 4, Hanns 1½ years.
2. Johannes *Müller*, Maria, have no children yet.
3. Theobald *Thiel*, Syngen, 4 children: Agnes 15, Hanns 13, Maria 8, Jonas 6 years.
4. Jung Hanns *Clos*, shoemaker, Margret, 8 children: Barbara 16, Mattheis 14, Klein Hans 12, Elisabeth 10, Hanns 8, Walpert 4, Appellonia 6, Johannes 2.

f. 197 v. 5. Nickel *Bergk*, Magdalena.
His son Philipps *Bergk* and his wife Catharina have a household of their own, and these young couple have 3 children: Margreth 6, Nickel 4 years, Abraham 13 weeks.
6. Hanns *Haffner*, Elisabeth, 4 children: Maria 9, Hanns 7, Clos 2, Engel 16 weeks.
7. Johannes *Schleich*, Engel, 2 children: Margret 5, Agnes 3. Is in the house of his father Peter Schleich(en).
8. Theobald *Knapff*, Walpert, 8 children: Agnes 18, Appellonia 16, Johannes 13, Clos 10, Theobald 8, Elisabeth 6, Jacob 4, Engel 1¼ years.

f. 198 9. Johannes *Schmucher*, censor, Margret, 4 children: Johannes 13, Hanns 10, Meckel 8, Junghanns 6.
10. Theobald *Knapff*, Engel, 2 children: Theobald 6, Hanns 1 year.
11. *Dietz*, cowherd, Catharina, 3 children: Syngen 5, Elisabeth 2, Maria 1 year.
12. Conrad *Schumacher*, Appellonia, 4 children: Hanns 20, Jacob 18, Theis 10, Maria 14 years.
13. Clos *Daub*, Appellonia, 3 children: Jacob 18, Walper 20, Margret 16.
14. Theis *Niderlender*, Agnes,[1] 4 children from his first wife: Hanns 18, Johannes 14, Theis 12, Antonius 4 years.
15. Hanns *Kampff*, Ela, have 1 child (name not stated).

f. 198 v. *Village Reheweiler.*[2]

1. Jonas *Karcher*, Eva, 7 children: Willrich 20, Barbara 14, Catharina 16, Theobald 12, Dieterich 8, Nickel 5, Hanns Wolf 3 years.
2. Hans *Müller*, Margret, 2 children: Hans 2½, Margret 1 year.
3. Junghanns *Müller*, Catharina, 2 children: Hanns 8, Ela 2½.

---

[1] His second wife, who had no children.

[2] Rehweiler on the Glan, south of Eisenbach.

4. Bastian *Crämer*, Catharina, 3 children: Catharina 5, Magdalena 3 years, Agnes 8 weeks.

5. Hanns *Jung*, Barbel, 4 children: Wilhelm 7, Jonas 4, Nickel 2 years, Johannes 8 weeks.

6. Hanns *Heinrich*, Margret, 4 children: Jacob 16, Margret 12, Johannes 8, Hanns 3 years.

f. 199   7. Dieterich *Bergk*, Margret, 1 daughter: Magdalena, 3 years.

8. Magdalena, Hanns *Kleinhardt'* widow, 5 children: Hans 28, Nickel 23, Eva 19, Barbara 13, Theobald 10 years, and Magdalena, a widow.

9. Mattheis *Metzler*, Catharina, are two old people and have no children.

f. 199 v.   *Hoff Liebenstall.*[1]

1. Jacob *Rintweiler*, Elisabeth, 5 children: Claus, Wilhelm, Elisabeth, Catharina, Margret.

2. Peter *Schleuch*, Maria, 1 child: Tilleman.

3. Hanns *Wüllenweber*, Catharina, 3 children: Margret, Barbara, Meckel.

4. Hanns *Theobald* the shepherd, Maria, 6 children: Barbel, Maria, Nickel, Maria, Symon, Niclaus.

5. Appellonia, *Peter's* widow, 6 orphans: Nickel, Job, Wilhelm, Clos, Maria, Catharina.

f. 200   *Village Traweiler.*[2]

1. Daniel *Knapf* (wife not named), 4 children: Eva 6, Maria 5, Catharina 4, Theobald 2 years.

2. Hanns *Drott* the old (wife not named), no children.

3. Johannes *Drott*, Elisabeth, 5 children: Nickel 8, Abraham 6, Nickel 4, Anna 3, Catharina 2 years.

4. *Schäffer* Johannes, Farina, nihil.

5. Johannes *Khühirdt*, Margret, 4 children: Johannes 8, Peter 6, Hanns Peter 4, Barbara 2 years.

6. Steffan *Jung*, Catharina, 3 children: Catharina 5, Maria 4, Peter 3 years.

f. 200 v.   7. Hanns *Scherer*, Elisabeth, fem. servant Catharina of Steinbach.

8. Nickel *Jung*, censor (wife not named), 4 children: Meckulda 16, Hanns 10, Barbara 7, Maria 3 years.

9. *Seymets* Merten, Catharina, 2 children: Claus 20, Hennsell 16 years.

10. Johannes *Lawer*, Margret, 4 children: Maria 6, Catharina 5, Johannes 3, Hanns 2 years.

11. Barbara, Jacob *Meurer's* widow, 2 children: Catharina 18, Maria 6 years.

---

[1] Liebsthal, west of Rehweiler.

[2] Trahweiler, south of Liebsthal.

Village Frutzweiler.[1]

1. *Jung* Clos, Catharina, no children, 1 male servant Abraham of Feckelbergk.
2. Nickel *Schneider*, Catharina, 3 children: Magdalena 23, Nickel 16, Conrad 15 years.
3. Catharina Bürtel *Kochen'* widow, 2 sons: Hans 24, Nickel 20 years.
4. *Allt* Theobald, Judith, neither children nor servants.
5. Peter *Becker*, Maria, 2 children: Peter 16, Nickel 14.
6. *Seimets* Bürtel, Appel, 2 children: Catharina 12, Maria 10 years.
7. *Schuch* Clos, Agnes, 2 children: Hanns 2, Nickel 1 year.
8. Hanns *Holgesser's* son-in-law, his wife Catharina, they have no children.

9. Bast *Schmidt*, Gertrud, 5 children: Margret 10, Peter 8, Hanns Peter 7, Hanns 6, Clos 4 years old.
10. Michel *Allt*, Margret, 4 children: Magdalen 10, Margret 8, Nickel 7, Hanns 3 years.
11. Kleinhanns *Bender*, Maria, 6 children: Eva 18, Nickel 16, Johannes 14, Clos 12, Catharina 10, Hanns 6 years.

---

[1] Frutzweiler on the Steinbach, southwest of Trahweiler.

LOCAL REGISTER.

The numbers refer to the pages of the original manuscript.

PERSONAL REGISTER.

EXPLANATION OF CHRISTIAN NAMES.

Andres, Anders	Andreas	Jöb	Jobst
Antes, Anthes	Anton	Jörg	Georg
Appel, Appellonia	Apollonia	Lena, Lehna	Helena
Barbel, Barbelichen	Barbara	Magdalen, Madlena	Magdalena
Bast, Bastian	Sebastian	Marei, Marey	Maria
Best, Besten	Sebastian	Mareylin	Maria
Birtel, Bürtel	Barthel	Margret, Margretichen	Margareta
Catrein, Catter,		Marten, Merten	Martin
Cathetter, Cetter,		Nesen	Agnes
Catereinichen	Catharina	Nickel, Niklas	Nikolaus
Christmann	Christian	Nicloss	Nikolaus
Clas, Clos	Nikolaus	Noll	Arnold
Deobalt	Theobald	Petter	Peter
Diebolt, Deboltgen	Debolt	Remig, Remmen	Remigius
Ehl, Ela, Els	Elisabeth	Seimet, Seimot	Simon
Enders, Enners	Andreas	Seymot	Simon
Ferena, Farina	Veronica	Sin, Sinn, Sinna	Euphrosine
Geham, Gehames	Johannes	Stoffel	Christoffel
Gehann, Gehannes	Johannes	Theiss, Theissen	Mattheis
Gerta, Gertta	Gertrude	Theus	Mattheus
Getz, Getza	Gesa	Thiel, Tiel, Tielman	Tilmann
Geetz, Getzen	Gesa	Trine, Trina	Catharina
Haman	Hermann	Utilia	Ottilia
Hanse, Hensel	Hans	Valtin, Veltin, Velten	Valentin
Haupert	Hubert	Varina, Värein	Veronica
Joan, Joes	Johannes	Wolff	Wolfgang
Joannes	Johannes		

REGISTER OF NAMES.

FAMILY NAMES: On account of varieties in spelling the seeker is advised to examine all variants in the Index thoroughly for the desired reference.

A.

Achtelsbacher,	Anna	159v
	Hans	159v
	Margreta	**159v**
	Maria	159v
	Peter	162
Acker,	Hans	164v
	Jacob	164v
	Johannes	164v
	Katharina ...	164v
	Nickel	164v
Adam,	Hans	162
	Margreta	162
zu Alben,	Margreta	51v
	Niclas	51v
Albert,	Claus	62
Albinus,	Catharina	47
	Johannes	47
Alles,	Aell	186v
	Christina	186v
	Christman	186v
	Dathein	186v
	Elisabeth	186v
	Johannes	186v
	Maria	186v
	Nikolaus	186v
	Wendel	186v
Allt,	Hanns	201v
	Judith	201
	Magdalena ...	201v
	Margreta	201v
	Michel	201v
	Nikolaus	201v
	Theobald	201
Alt,	Catharina..14,	152v
	Jacob	14
	Johannes	8
	Sara	8
	Thomas	152v

Althanns,	Barthel	128v
	Gertrud	128v
	Johannes	128v
	Margreta	128v
	Nikolaus	128v
Anstat,	Apollonia	31
	Bernhard	31
	Gertraud	31
	Magdalena ...	31
Anthes,	Elisabeth	66
	Nikolaus	66
Anthess,	Heinrich	16v
	Margretha ...	16v
Anthoni,	Henrich	159v
	Peter	159v
Apel,	Hans	129v
	Margreta	129v
	Nikolaus	129v
Appel,	Barbara	80v
	Grete	80v
	Hans	188
	Katharina....	188
Appeln,	Adam	188
	Debolt	188
	Elisabeth	188
	Engel	188
	Maria	188
	Nikolaus	188
Arets zu Kreen-Nest,		
	Antes	80
	Barbara	80
	Geza	80
	Peter	80
Arnold,	Johannes	169
	Margreta	169
	Sara	169
	Sibilla	169
	Stoffel	169

Arweiler,	Catharina	106	Bär,	Barbara	75
	Johannes	106		Hanns	75
	Margreta	106		Hans Georg	75
	Maria Salome.	106		Hans Nikolaus	75
Aulenbacher,	Margreta	6	Barbel,	Agnes	129
	Peter	6		Barthel	129
Aysell,	Barbara	66		Gertrud	129
	Clauss	66		Hans	129
	Johannes	66		Johannes	129
	Katharina	66		Margreta	129
				Martin	129
B.				Simon	129
Baal,	Daniel	109	Barben,	Adam	49
	Hanns	109		Margreta	49
	Hans Martin	109	Barborn,	Eva	48v
	Margreta	109		Maria	48
Bach,	Engel	184v		Tobias	48
	Jacob	184v	Bart,	Anna	79v
	Johannes	184v		Antes	79v
Backers,	Bernhard	49v		Barbara	79v
	Catharina	49v		Hubert	79v
Bahl,	Johannes	7		Jacob	79v
	Margreta	7		Catharina	79v
Baier,	Clara	41v		Maria	79v
	Hans	41v		Michel	79v
Bair,	Abraham	160		Nikolaus	79v
	Anna	160		Sinn	79v
	Anna Grete	160	Bartel,	Adelheid	166
	Barbara	163v		Apollonia	165v
	Daniel	160		Elisabeth	165v
	Elisabet	163v		Hans	166
	Hans	163v		Jung Hansen	165v
	Hans Jost	160		Martha	166
	Hans Nikolaus	160		Nicolaus	166
	Jacob	163v		Otilia	166
	Katharina	163v	Bartholome,	Hans Daniel	159v
	Magdalena	163v		Elisabeth	159v
	Maria	163v		Stoffel	159v
	Maria Salome	160	Bartz,	Abraham	24
	Tobias	160		Catharina	24
	Ursula	160		Elisabeth	24
Baldwen,	Anna	105		Herman	24
	Maria Magdalena	105		Johannes	24
				Maria	24
Bär,	Apollonia	75	Bast,	Anna	64
				Closs	188, 79v

Becker, Closs 31v, 74, 126
Daniel 31v
Elisabeth
31v, 74, 75, 160, 184v
Engel 14, 74, 106, 126
Esther 13v
Eva 40, 75, 125v
Hans ...31v, 40, 75, 125v,
126, 133, 162, 168v, 186
Hans Daniel 162
Hans Nickel 160
Hans Wilhelm 126
Jacob 48
Jobst (Jöb) 75
Jochim 184v
Johannes..7v, 14, 24, 31v,
40, 106, 125v, 160, 184,
184v, 186
Jonas 6, 13
Junghans 159
Katharina 64, 75, 162, 184
Lucia 17
Margareta...6, 12, 13, 24,
31v, 75, 106, 125v, 126,
133, 168v, 184, 184v, 186
Maria....14, 16, 31v, 40,
74, 159, 186, 201
Martha 31v, 161v
Mattheis (Theis) ... 64
Metz 184v
Michel 74, 126, 152v
Nickel....12, 125v, 152v,
184, 201
Niklas, Niklaus
82, 106, 186
Noa 17
Ottilie 160
Nohe 6
Peter...75, 162, 184v, 201
Sebastian 24, 106
Sophie 75
Stoffel 75
Theobald 16

Beckers, Abraham 161v
Johannes 161v
Junghans 161v
Margreta 161v

Beiel, Antonius 24
Catharina 24

Beiel, Elisabeth 24
Maria 24
Tillmann 24

Beier, Apollonia 63
Barbara 63
Catharina 63
Elisabeth 63
Hans 63
Hans Peter .. 63
Johannes 63
Maria 63
Nikolaus 63

Beller, Daniel 28v/29
Elisabeth ..28v/29
Hans 28v/29
Johann 28v/29

Bender, Agnes 27, 184
Catharina 201v
Closs 201v
Elizabeth 184
Eva 201v
Geza 41
Gertraud 66
Hans 27, 201v
Jacob 27
Johannes 27, 41, 201v
Margret 184
Maria 201v
Martin 66
Nikolaus ..41, 201v
Philippa 64
Theobald 41
Wendell 64

Berg, Johannes 27
Martha 27
Veronica 27

Bergk, Abraham 197v
Catharina 197v
Dieterich 198v
Magdalena
197v, 198v
Margreth 197v, 198v
Nikolaus 197v
Philipp 197v

Bernhard, Anna 31
Anstat 31
Apollonia 31
Catharina 31

Bössharen,	Johannes	.... 167v	Bueb,	Debolt	...... 164v
	Katharina	... 167v		Elisabeth (Els)	
Braun,	Balthasar	 162			164, 164v
	Elisabeth	 63		Engel	 164
	Elsa	.... 48v		Haman	 164
	Hans	 63		Hans	 164
	Jobst (Job)	.. 109		Katharina	... 164
	Margreta	 162		Margreta	 164
	Maria	 109		Sara	.... 164v
	Nikolaus	.... 48v		Sebastian	.... 164v
Braunhans,	Barbara	 47	Buhl,	Jakob	 152
				Margreta	 152
Brecher,	Margreta	 47	Bul,	Catharina	 50
	Nikolaus	 47		Cunrad (Con-	
Bretter,	Ottilia	...... 49v		rad)	 50
	Peter	.... 49v		Elisabeth	 50
				Johann	 50
Broch,	Agnes	 133		Margreta	 50
	Hans (Hensgen)	133		Nikolaus	 50
	Johannes	 133			
	Maria	 133	Bull,	Margreta	 63
	Nikolaus (Nickel)	133		Nikolaus	 63
Bron,	Adam	 63	Bungert,	Agnes	.... 76v
				Christina	.... 76v
Bruch,	Apollonia	 66		Closs	.... 76v
	Barbara	..... 184v		Jacob	.... 76v
	Hans Jacob	.. 184v		Johannes	.... 76v
	Thomas	....66, 184v		Sin	.... 76v
				Susanna	..... 76v
Bruder,	Elisabeth	 50			
	Hans	 162	Burg,	Eva	 81
	Hans Valentin	162		Imch	 81
	Johannes	 162			
	Jost	 162	Bürtel,	Anna	 31
	Magdalena	... 162		Catharina	 31
	Margreta	 162		Conrad	 31
	Martin (Merten)	50		Hans	 31
				Johannes	 31
Bub,	Daniel	 7		Margreta	 31
	Elisabeth (Elss)	7		Peter	 31
	Jacob	 15		vergl. Bietel	
	Katharina	... 160			
	Margreta	 15	Busch,	Apollonia	 82
				Engel	 82
Buch,	Elisabeth (Elss)	76		Johannes	 82
	Engel	 76		Margreta	 82
	Eva	 76		Martha	 82
	Hans	 76		Nikolaus	 82
	Henrich	 76		Simon (Seimet)	82
Bueb,	Agnes	 164	Buttel,	Catharina	.... 12v
	Bastian	...... 164v		Jonas	.... 12v

Buttel,	Johannes 12v	
	Engel 12v	
Büttel,	Adam 187v	
	Adam Heilman 129v	
	Agnes 129v	
	Anna 40v	
	Barbara 40	
	Catrina 40v	
	Christina 129v	
	Conrad 40v	
	Daniel 40v	
	Elisabeth 129v	
	Eva 40v, 187	
	Gertta 187	
	Hanns 129v	
	Johannes 40v,	
	129v, 187	
	Margreta 40v,	
	129v, 187	
	Nikolaus 129v	
	Peter 40, 40v	

C.

Cappel,	Adam 13v	
	Daniel 13v	
	Eva 13v	
	Susanna 13v	
Cappes,	Apollonia 49	
	Franz 49	
Cardio,	Ludwig 152v	
	Margreta 152v	
Carius,	Catharina 12v	
	Johannes ..12v, 13	
Caspar,	Barbara 63	
	Barnhard 48v	
	Cathrina 50, 63	
	Elisabeth (Elss) 76v	
	Hans 76v	
	Jacob 50	
	Maria 48v, 63	
	Nickel 63, 76v	
Censs,	Peter 25v	
	Sara 25v	
Christman,	Agnes 187	
	Hans 76	
	Johannes 76	
	Katrina (Trina) 76	

Christman,	Maria 76	
	Hans Michel .. 76	
Christmann,	Johann 8	
	Sara 8	
Chuno,	Abraham 27v/28	
	Barbara 27v/28	
	Catharina ..27v/28	
	Clos 27v/28	
	Elisabeth ...27v/28	
	Jacob 27v/28	
	Maria 27v/28	
	Sara 27v/28	
Clas,	Barbara ..152v, 162	
	Catharina ...63, 165	
	Conrad 164	
	Dilman 63	
	Gehannes 63	
	Gesa (Getza) . 168	
	Hans 168	
	Hans Michel .. 160	
	Hans Nickel .. 160	
	Hans Peter ... 63	
	Johannes ...63, 168	
	Ketichen 162	
	Margreta	
	162, 164, 168	
	Maria 160	
	Nickel 63, 161v, 164	
	Peter 160	
	Simon 165	
	Tillmann 63	
Class,	Bernhard 167	
	Elisabeth (Els) 167	
	Franz 167	
	Peter 167	
Claus,	Clara 62	
	Hans 62	
	Johannes 62	
	Margreta 50	
	Nikolaus 62	
	Peter 62	
Clauss,	Apollonia 51v	
	Elisabeth 16v	
	Elsa 47	
	German 16v	
	Margreta 16v	
	Wilhelm 47	

Cleburg,	Dionisius 77v	
	Magdalena ... 77v	
Clein,	Elias 28v/29	
	Jacob ...24, 28v/29	
	Johannes 24, 28v/29	
	Margreta ...28v/29	
	Maria 24	
	Martha 28v/29	
	vergl. Klein	
Clesich,	Katharina 163	
Clintzg,	Abraham 24v	
	Catharina 24v	
	Elisabeth 24v	
	Hans 24v	
	Johannes 24v	
	vergl. Klintz	
Clintzinger,	*see* Clintzg ... 24v	
Clos,	Abraham 82	
	Anna 82	
	Apollonia 82	
	Barbara 82	
	Bast (Sebastian) 82	
	Clara 82	
	Eva 82	
	Hans 82	
	Jacob 82	
	Johannes 82	
	Jost 82	
	Katharina 82	
	Margreta 82	
	Maria 82	
	Michel 82	
	Peter 82	
	Thomas 82	
Closen,	Catharina 48	
	Hans 48	
Closs,	Apollonia 197	
	Barbara 197	
	Elisabeth 197	
	Hans 197	
	Johannes 197	
	Margreta 197	
	Mattheiss 197	
	Walpert 197	
Clunt,	Barbara 162	
	Daniel 162	
	Hans Jacob ... 162	

Clunt,	Margreta 162	
Colman,	Agnes 63	
	vergl. Kolman . 63	
Conen,	Jacob 62	
Contzen,	Debolt 167v	
	Katharina ... 167v	
Cornelius,	Agnes 195	
	Anna 195	
	Barbara 195	
	Christina 195	
	Elisabeth 195	
	Johannes 195	
	Maria 195	
	Meckuldta 195	
	Wilhelm 195	
Correts,	Anna 78	
	Bast (Sebastian) 78	
	Hans 78	
	Maria 78	
	Peter 78	
Coster,	Conrad 16	
	Maria 16	
	Katharina 16	
Crämer,	Agnes 198v	
	Bastian 198v	
	Catharina 198v	
	Magdalena ... 198v	
	vergl. Krämer	
Cräss,	Maria 65	
	Nikolaus 65	
Cratz,	Barbara 24, 24v	
	Catharina 24v	
	Engel 24v	
	Gesa (Getza).. 24	
	Hans 24v	
	Jacob 24v	
	Johannes 24	
	Margreta 24	
Creutz,	Catharina 195v	
	Elisabeth 195v	
	Engel 195v	
	Hans 195v	
	Jacob 195	
	Johannes 195v	
	Margret 195	
	Maria 195v	

Gros,	Johannes 161v	Haas,	Engel 126
	Margreta 161v		Johannes ...25v, 126
Gross,	Catharina 13, 24		Margrete ...25v, 126
	Christina 188		Maria 126
	Elisabet (Els) .. 188		Ottilia 126
	Engel 152		Peter 51
	Hans 152, 188	Hafener,	Apollonia 41v
	Johannes 24		Cathrine 41v
	Margrete 188		Daniel 41v
	Nikolaus 188		Hans 41v
Grub,	Nikolaus 64		Maria 41v
			Matthias 41v
Grüb,	Johannes 66		Ursula 41v
	Margrete 66	Haffner,	Closs 197v
Grum,	Barbara 160		Elisabeth 197v
	Hans Peter 160		Engel 197v
	Hans Wolfgang. 160		Hanns 197v
	Maria Salome .. 160		Maria 197v
Gruman,	Hanns 126	Hafner,	Barbara 168
	Margrete 126		Elisabet (Els) .. 168
	Nikolaus 126		Nikolaus 168
Gudendahl	Anna 75		Sara 168
	Christina 75	Hainsell,	Closs 152
	Engel 75		Hans 152
	Hans 75		Kinigin 152
	Margreta 75		Margreta 152
	Maria 75	Haintz,	Agnes 168v
	Peter 75		Andreas 168v
	Sinna 75		Anna 160v
Günterod, von			Johannes 168v
	Albrecht 105		Margreta 168v
	Friedrich		Paulus 160v
	Casimir 105	Hainz,	Elisabeth (Elss) 65
	Hans Wolfgang. 105		Ludwig 65
	Maria Magdalena 105	Haisel,	Anna 40
Gutscher,	Anna 107		Jacob 40
	Apollonia 105		Johannes 40
	Catharina 105		Maria 40
	Hans 105	Haman,	Barbara 49
	Herman 105		Hans 49
	Johannes 105		Maria (Marei) .. 7
	Magdalena 105		Peter 49
	Nikolaus 105	Hamel,	Gertraud 48
H.			Johann 48
Haas,	Anna 126	Hamman,	Catharina 124
	Barbara 126		Jost 124
	Catharina 51, 126		

Heerman,	Peter	160v
	Tobias	160v
Heilman,	Abraham 159, 165	
	Agnes	165
	Adam	49v
	Apollonia	49v
	Barbara 51, 152	
	Bastian	165
	Brigitta	195
	Closs	81
	Elisabeth 81, 164, 165	
	Hans 81, 152	
	Margreta	
	152, 159, 165, 195	
	Meckulda	159
	Nikolaus **164, 195**	
	Ottilia 159, 195	
	Sebastian	165
	Simon ..159, 164, 195	
	Theobald	195
Heinrich,	Hanns	198v
	Jacob	198v
	Johannes	198v
	Margrete	198v
Heinsel,	Cornelius	187v
	Jacob	187v
	Johannes	187v
	Margrete	187v
Heintz,	Catharina	48
	Daniel	163v
	Elisabeth	50
	Johannes 48, 50	
	Margreta	163v
	Nikolaus	50
Heisel,	Anna	108
	Johannes	108
	Margrete	108
	Nikolaus	108
	Simon (Seimet) .	108
	Theobald	108
Helbgewachss,		
	Christina	152
	Ruprecht	152
Helfant,	Anna	105
Helffenstein,		
	Anna	125

Helffenstein,		
	Albertus	125
	Benjamin	125
	Hans Wilhelm ..	125
	Johan Anastasius	125
	Johan Andreas..	125
	Johan Chrisos-	
	tomus	125
	Johan Friedrich.	125
	Johan ..106, 125, 194	
	Kunigundis	106
Hell,	Barbara	187
	Johannes	187
	Katharine	187
	Michel	187
Hellriegel,	Anna	160v
	Anna Elisabet ..	160v
	Barbara	160v
	Daniel	160v
	Gallus	160v
	Hans Daniel	160v
	Katharina	160v
	Künigund	160v
Helpescher,	Engel	50
	Nikolaus	50
Helpeschner,		
	Elisabeth	49v
	Johann	49v
Helrigel,	Anna	31
	Barbara	31v
	Catharina	31
	Engel	31
	Gallus	31
	Jacob	31
	Johann	31v
	Margreta	31
	Maria	31
	Michel	31
	Nikolaus	31
Hengen,	Catharina	152v
	Closs	152v
Henness,	Gertrud	49v
	Hans	49v
Hennessen,	Barbara	165
	Hans	165
	Margreta	165
	Wilhelm	165

Hök,	Johannes	47		**J.**		
	Margreta	47	Jacob,	Barbara	74	
	see Hock			Elisabeth (Elss)	74	
Holgesser,	Catharina	201		Hans	74	
	Hanns	201	Jacoby,	Barbara	63	
Holz,	Henrich	40		Johannes	63	
	Herman	40		Maria	63	
	Ilsebeth	40		Nikolaus	63	
	Maria	40		Sebastian	63	
	Nikolaus	40	Jeckel,	Elisabeth	50	
	Simon	40		Elsa	48v	
Horch,	Elisabeth (Elss)	76		Engel	50	
	Georg (Jörg)	76		Matthias	50	
	Hans	76		Wilhelm	50	
Horrenberger,			Jerusalem,	Agnes	168	
	Christman	75		Clas	168	
	Clara	75		Engel	168	
	Elisabeth (Elss)	75		Hans	168	
	Hans	75		Henrich	168	
	Hans Jacob	75	Jmch,	Barbara	83	
	Nikolaus	75		Katharina	83	
Höt,	Barbara	82		Nikolaus	83	
	Jacob	82	Joachim,	Apollonia	186	
Höwe,	Agnes	187	Jochim,	Agnes	186	
	Christina	187		Hans	186	
	Eva	187				
	Hans Jacob	187	Jöckel,	Catharina	7	
	Nikolaus	187		David	7	
Hübsch,	Anna	17		Eva	7	
	Jacob	17		Michael	7	
Hüel,	Anna	184	Johannes,	Maria	47	
	Barbara	184	Johannet,	Elisabeth (Els)	187v	
	Engel	184		Katharina	187v	
	Gertrud (Gert)	184	Joichims,	Gesa (Getza)	49v	
	Hans (Hensgen)	184		Hans	49v	
	Hubert (Haupert)	184				
	Johannes	184	Jonas,	Maria	51v	
	Nikolaus	184	Jörg,	Agnes	81	
Huttmacher,				Anna	79v	
	Adam	184		Closs	81	
	Hans	184		Elisabeth (Elss)	81	
	Margreta	184		Fritz	81	
	I.			Hans	81	
Isaac,	Adelheid	186v		Johannes	79v	
	Magdalena	186v		Nikolaus	79v, 81	
	Sara	186v		Sinn	78v	

Loch,	Gerat	130v
	Ilsebeth	41v
	Johannes	130v
	Jonas	41
	Maria 41, 130v	
Lohwer,	Anna	47
	Michel	47
Lorch, Lork,	Abraham	15
	Caspar	66
	Catharina	15
	Maria	66
Lorck,	Elisabeth	15
	Johannes	15
Lorentz,	Abraham	7
	Closs	80
	Elisabeth (Ehl).	78
	Engel	78
	Johannes	78
	Katharine	78
	Martha	7
	Peter	78
Lorenz,	Anna	63
	Catharina	63
	Elisabeth	63
	Johann (Geham)	63
	Maria	63
	Nikolaus	63
	Peter	63
Lork,	Abraham	15
	Catherina	15
Lower,	Anton (Antoin).	47
	Catharina	47
Luder,	Apollonia	74
	Engel	74
	Hans	74
	Johannes	74
	Jörg (Georg) ..	74
	Margrete	74
	Maria	74
	Nikolaus	74
Ludwig,	Agnes	129v
	Barthel	129v
	Margrete	129v
	Theobald	129v
Lutt,	Johannes	47
	Ottilia	47

M.

Mack,	Abraham 14, 15	
	Barbara	14
	Catharina	15
	David	14
	Eva	14
	Hans	14
Mackh,	Johann	51v
	Veronica (Ferena)	51v
Mair,	Anna	168
	Elisabeth ...162, 166	
	Hans	162
	Hans Abraham..	162
	Hans Martin ...	162
	Hans Nikolaus ..	162
	Hans Peter	162
	Johannes 162,166,168	
	Katharine	168
	Margreta ...166, 168	
	Maria	162
	Martha	166
	Nikolaus	166
	Peter	166
Malzbacher,	Agnes	125v
	Closs	125v
Mann,	see Kleinmann..	7
Martin,	Anna	40
	Barbara 40, 47	
	Cathrina	40
	Daniel	40
	David	165v
	Elisabeth	50
	Hans	40
	Ilsebeth	40
	Johann	50
	Johannat	165v
	Margrete	40
	Maria	7v
	Theobald	40
Marx,	Anna	161
	Katharina	161
	Matthes	161
Mattes,	Apollonia	83
	Closs	83
	Hans	83
	Johannes	83
	Maria	83

Niderländer, Agnes 168
          Elisabeth (Els). 168
          Hubert
            (Haupert) ... 168
          Philip 168

Niderlender, Agnes 198
          Antonius 198
          Hanns 198
          Johannes 198
          Mattheiss
            (Theiss) 198

Niklas,   Margreta 64

Niliessen, Ilse 40v

Nofelser, Barbara 74
          Michel 74
Noper,   Elisabeth 51
          Johann 51

O.

Oedinger, Catharina 24
          Johannes 24

Offerbacher, Johannes 7v

Olien,   Abraham 16v
          Sara 16v

Oliger,   Maria 16v
          Michael 16v

Opin,   Katharina 163

Opp,   Christina 106
          Eva 106
          Hans Siefried .. 106
          Jacob 106

Ort,   Nikolaus 51
Otilie,   Barbara 51v
          Nikolaus 51v

P.

Palm,   Barbara 31v
          Kaul 31v
Paulus,   Catharina 152v
          Hans 152

Paulussen, Barbara 107
          Elisabeth 107
          Jacob 107
          Johannes 107
          Martha 107

Peil,   Catharina 8v
          Johannes 8v

Peter,   Abraham 40v
          Anna 40v, 52, 64
          Apollonia 199v
          Barthel 132, 165
          Caspar 64
          Catharina
            16v, 50, 63, 168, 199v
          Clas, Closs...168, 199v
          Daniel 40v
          Elisa 63
          Elisabeth (Els)
            24, 63, 165, 168
          Eva 132
          Francisca 165
          Gertrud 132
          Hans..40v, 63, 64, 77,
            132, 165, 168
          Ilsebeth 40v
          Jacob 24
          Jobst (Job) ... 199v
          Johannes 6, 16v,
            40v, 50, 63, 165
          Jonas 40v
          Margreta..6, 165, 168
          Maria 24, 40v, 77, 199v
          Maria Salome... 24
          Martin 77
          Matthes 77
          Michel 77
          Nikolaus 132, 199v
          Peter 63
          Sibilla 165
          Wilhelm 199v

Peters,   Agnes 165
          Barbara 165
          Hans 165
          Katharein 165
          Sebastian
            (Bastian) ... 165

Petri,   Antonius 24
          Apollonia 31v
          Catharina 24
          Daniel 24, 31v
          Engel 13v
          Hans 31v
          Jacob 31v
          Jeremias 13v

Petri,	Johann	31v
	Jonas	24
	Magdalena	31v
	Maria	24
	Peter	31v
Petter,	Abraham	152v
	Elisabeth (Elss)	80v
	Johannes	80v
	Margreta	80v, 152v
Pettges,	Engel	6
Pfaff,	Christina	29v/30
	Johann	29v/30
Pfeiffer,	Agathe	126
	Agnes	126
	Hanns	13, 126
	Johannes	126
	Margreta	13
	Maria	126
	Martin	126, 165v
	Reinhard	126
Pfeil,	Anna Margrete	124v
	Elisabeth	48, 124v
	Johann	48, 124v
	Kunigunde	124v
	Maria Agnes	124v
Philip,	Apollonia	52
Philipp,	Agnes	187v
	Dathein	187v
	Demut	187v
	Margrete	187v
	Maria	187v
	Veit	187v
Philips,	Catharina	51
Piess,	Andreas(Andries)	50
	Anna	50
	Hans	50
Platz,	Anna	65
	Paulus	65
Poel,	Anna	27v/28
	Daniel	27v/28
	Elias	27v/28
	Johannes	27v/28
	Nikolaus	27v/28
Pohtt,	Apollonia	16
	Elisabeth	12v

Pohtt,	Hans	12v
	Johannes	16
Poland,	Apollonia	162
Popp,	Agnes	162
	Anna	162
	Anna Mädichen	162
	Conrad	162
	Jacob	162
Pot,	Anna	28v/29
	Catharina	28v/29
	Daniel	28v/29
	Hans	28v/29
	Jacob	28v/29
	Johann	28v/29
	Martha	28v/29
Pott,	Abraham	24
	Antonius	24
	Catharina	24
	Elizabeth	13
	Hans	13
	Maria	24
	Sebastian	24
Preud,	Abraham	24v
	David	24v
	Magdalena	24v
	Margreta	24v
	Meinhard	24v
Preuel,	Abraham	12
	Anna	24
	Catharina	24
	Elias	24
	Engel	12
	Margrete	24
Prewell,	Catharina	25v
	Johannes	25v
	Philipp	25v
Pulvermacher,		
	Agnes	185v
	Albrecht	185v
	Baschen	185v
	Hans Jacob	185v
	Heinrich	185v

Q.

| Queck, | Abraham | 164 |
| | Agnes | 164 |